Guide to Tourist Railroads and Railroad Museums

COMPILED BY GEORGE H. DRURY

Editor: Bob Hayden   Researcher and Copy Editor: Marcia Stern
Editorial Secretary: Monica Borowicki   Art Director: Lawrence Luser

On the cover: Northern Pacific Ten-Wheeler 328, an S-10-class machine built by American Locomotive Company's Rogers works in 1907 — reportedly designed and built for Russia but never shipped — leads a Minnesota Transportation Museum excursion train out of Lake Elmo, Minn., east of St. Paul, on Chicago & North Western rails on July 23, 1983. Photo by Robert M. Ball.

KALMBACH BOOKS

INTRODUCTION

Tourist railroads and railroad museums don't have a long history — most are creations of the past three decades. Until about 1950 you didn't need tourist railroads: If you wanted to ride a train, you went down to the station; if you wanted to see old cars and locomotives, you just looked around — thanks to the Depression, when the railroads couldn't afford new rolling stock, and World War Two, when the railroads needed every piece they could find, there was plenty to see. Then diesels replaced steam locomotives. Passenger trains were discontinued. Lines were abandoned. As it became more and more difficult to see or ride trains, more and more people said, "They were interesting" and "They were fun to ride."

And that, quite simply, is what railroad museums and tourist railroads are about. They preserve some of the most fascinating machinery mankind has ever devised, and they re-create an enjoyable aspect of the past — and if fascination and enjoyment aren't enough, no other industry is so intimately tied to the history and development of North America.

This book is arranged alphabetically by state, with Canada's provinces following the U. S., then Mexico; within states and provinces the attractions are listed alphabetically by town or city. The index at the back of the book lists the museums and railroads alphabetically by name.

For each museum and railroad there is a brief description; a row of symbols for features such as parking, accessibility to the handicapped, gift shop and bookstore, food service, and picnic area; and a quick-look table showing:

Locomotives	Quantity and types of locomotives operating on the railroad
Cars	Types of cars used to carry passengers
Displays	Non-operating equipment on display
Dates open	Seasons, days, and times the property is open to visitors
Schedule	Seasons, days, and times the trains operate
Admission	Price of entering the museum
Fares	Price to ride the train
Memberships	How you can become a member of the museum or the sponsoring organization
Nearby attractions	Other tourist attractions nearby that the family might enjoy
Address	Mailing address
Phone	Area code and number for the railroad or museum, plus other numbers for recorded information or for special locations

Unless otherwise credited, the photos were provided by the museums and the railroads.

A few known tourist railroads and railroad museums had to be left out for want of sufficiently detailed information. I will try to include them in subsequent editions. I welcome updated information and information on new railroads and museums.

Thanks are due to Nick Kallas, general manager of the Illinois Railway Museum, for his help in drafting the questionnaire to send to the museums and railroads, and to Judy Sandberg, Corresponding Secretary of TRAIN, the Tourist Railway Association, Inc. Special thanks go to Marcia Stern and Monica Borowicki for gathering the information for this book. Without their efforts this guide could not have been compiled.

GEORGE H. DRURY

Milwaukee, Wisconsin
January 1987

Locomotives	Diesel, usually GP40-2s and GP38s
Cars	Anchorage-Fairbanks: reclining-seat coaches, dome coaches, diners, snack bar/lounge cars; Anchorage-Seward: RDCs (Rail Diesel Cars)
Display	On display in parking lot at Anchorage depot is the 1915 steam locomotive used to construct the railroad.
Schedule	May 23-September 13, 1987: Anchorage-Denali Park-Fairbanks, daily: leave Anchorage and Fairbanks midmorning, about 10 hours; Anchorage-Seward, leaving Anchorage 7:30 a.m. Friday, Saturday, and Sunday, returning to Anchorage at 9:00 p.m. Additional local services are offered. Winter-season (September-May) service is considerably reduced.
Fares	Vary with trip. Anchorage-Fairbanks, $85 one way. Anchorage-Seward, $53 round trip. Children 5-11 half fare; under 5 free. Age 65 and up 50 percent discount mid-September through mid-May. Credit cards and checks accepted. Group discounts and charters available. Tickets and reservations are available through travel agents. In addition, several tour operators offer deluxe service.
Address	Passenger Services Department, 421 West 1st Avenue, P. O. Box 7-2111, Anchorage, AK 99510-7069
Phone	(800) 554-0552, (907) 265-2494

ALASKA RAILROAD CORPORATION

The Alaska Railroad, owned by the state of Alaska, was completed in 1923. It is a full-size, common-carrier railroad offering freight and passenger service. It is included in this book because most of its passenger service is aimed at the tourist. The line stretches 470 miles from Seward through Anchorage and past Mount McKinley to Fairbanks, and there is a 12-mile branch from Portage to Whittier. It is a mountainous line, traveling through some of the most rugged and remote scenery in North America, including Mount McKinley. The Seward line passes glaciers, hangs at one point on top of a canyon wall, and uses four tunnels within one mile to get up the mountain.

Reservations are mandatory for the Anchorage-Fairbanks trains and Anchorage-Seward excursions. The Anchorage and Fairbanks offices have staff on hand year-round. Each train carries a full-service, sit-down dining car, with all meals prepared on board.

Anchorage

Locomotives	3 steam, 2 diesel (5/12 scale)
Cars	5/12-scale gondola and cattle cars
Displays	Full-size engine, baggage car, Pullman car, railroad antiques, 2 railroad stations, 3 model railroads, live steam club
Schedule	Monday-Friday 10 a.m. to dusk. Weekends 11 a.m. to dusk.
Fares	Age 3 and up 50 cents (under 3 free). Checks accepted. Tuesday-Friday mornings $15 per trip for groups with reservations.
Memberships	$20 per year, Scottsdale Railroad & Mechanical Society
Special events	Concerts (March, June, July); Railfair (October); holiday lights (December); Exclusively Little (February)
Address	7301 East Indian Bend Road, Scottsdale, AZ 85253
Phone	(602) 994-2312

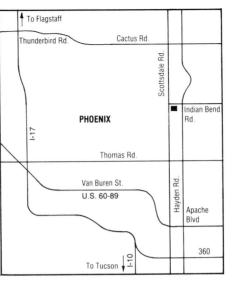

McCORMICK RAILROAD PARK

McCormick Railroad Park is a 30-acre, railroad-theme park at the southeast corner of Scottsdale and Indian Bend Road in Scottsdale, Arizona. It has been operated by the city of Scottsdale Recreation Division since 1975.

The Paradise & Pacific features a 1-mile, 8-minute ride through the park on 15″ gauge track aboard a 5/12-scale gondola or cattle car. All rolling stock is modeled after Rio Grande Southern or Denver & Rio Grande Western equipment.

Model railroad clubs have O, HO, and N scale layouts for public viewing, and a live steam club provides free rides Sundays on its ¾″, 1″, and 1½″ scale equipment. Full-size equipment on display includes a 1907 2-6-0 Baldwin steam engine; 1914 Santa Fe baggage car; and the luxury Pullman car *Roald Amundsen*, built in 1928 and used by visiting dignitaries and U. S. presidents. Two railroad stations — the Peoria, built in 1894, and the Aguila, built in 1907 — house railroad memorabilia shops.

A special birthday party package is available at the park; make reservations well in advance. Three picnic pavilions, available with reservations, will accommodate groups; other picnic areas are on a first-come, first-served basis. The park also has a volleyball court, playgrounds, and grass playing fields. The grounds are accessible to handicapped or people with baby strollers.

Locomotives	3 steam, 1 diesel
Cars	2 coaches, 1 gondola, 1 caboose
Schedule	Daily, mid-April through October. Departures, rain or shine, hourly from 10 a.m. to 4 p.m. Charter trips available.
Fares	Adults $5.00. Children 5-12 $2.50 (under 5 free). Discounts for groups of 20 or more. Credit cards and checks accepted.
Special events	Civil War reenactment, Railfest
Nearby attractions	Great Passion play, country music shows
Address	P. O. Box 310, Eureka Springs, AR 72632
Phone	(501) 253-9623, 253-9677

EUREKA SPRINGS & NORTH ARKANSAS RAILWAY

Established in 1980, the Eureka Springs & North Arkansas operates from a stone depot at 299 North Main Street (Highway 23 North and Eureka Springs city limits). Visitors may park at the depot, ride the steam train, then ride the trolley through historic downtown Eureka Springs. The trolley stops at the depot approximately every 30 minutes.

The train travels 2 miles north from the depot to the old mainline junction, then returns, a 45-minute round trip through the Ozark Mountain countryside in northern Arkansas. The line, formerly part of the Missouri & North Arkansas, was originally built in 1883.

The ES&NA grounds are accessible to handicapped or people with baby strollers, and there are two acres of level recreational vehicle parking. Staff is on the premises year-round, and restaurants and lodging are available in Eureka Springs.

The *Eurekan*, a fully restored vintage dining car, serves three meals per day; reservations are required for trips in the diner. A Christmas Dining Car Special is planned for the Thanksgiving through Christmas season.

Eureka Springs

ARKANSAS-5

Locomotives	2 steam
Cars	Wood and steel coaches
Equipment on display	Freight and passenger cars
Schedule	May: Saturday at 11 a.m. and 2 p.m.; Sunday at 2 p.m. Memorial Day through mid-August: Thursday-Saturday at 11 and 2; Sunday at 2. Mid-August through October: Sunday at 2. Rain or shine.
Fares	Adults $5.00. Children 4-11 $3.00 (under 4 free). Credit cards accepted. Discounts for groups of 15 or more reserving one week in advance. Charters available for a minimum of 70 adults.
Special events	Spring and fall night runs. Holiday events include Civil War reenactments and train robberies.
Nearby attractions	Crater of Diamonds State Park, White Oak Lake State Park, Old Washington Historic State Park, Hot Springs National Park
Address	Reader Industries, Inc., 803 Cabe Street, P. O. Box 9, Malvern, AR 72104
Phone	(501) 337-9591 (office), 685-2692 (depot, weekends May-October)

READER RAILROAD

This historic logging line, founded in 1889 by A. S. Johnson, is the oldest all-steam, standard gauge, common carrier railroad in North America. The wood-burning locomotive and its train depart from the depot on Highway 368 in the old mill town of Reader, just off Highway 24 between Camden and Prescott, Arkansas. It travels 3½ miles from the depot to the logging camp at Camp DeWoody, then returns, a 1 hour and 20 minute round trip through hilly woodlands.

The 40-acre grounds are accessible to handicapped or people with baby strollers. Guided tours are offered by reservation, and staff is in the office at Malvern year-round. Restaurants and lodging are available in nearby Camden and Prescott.

Special night trains, originating at Camp DeWoody, feature dinner at Adams Crossing and live bluegrass and country music. Write for a brochure and reservation form.

Bob Hayden

Displays	Southern Pacific 4-6-0; 7 cars; 1883 depot
Dates open	Daily, March 15-November 15, 10 a.m. to 4 p.m.
Admission	Free, but donations are accepted.
Memberships	Memberships in Bishop Museum & Historical Society available.
Nearby attractions	Hunting, fishing, camping, and skiing in High Sierras.
Address	P. O. Box 363, Bishop, CA 93514
Phone	(619) 873-5950

LAWS RAILROAD MUSEUM & HISTORICAL SITE

From 1943 to 1960 Laws, California, was the northern terminal of Southern Pacific's narrow gauge line through the Owens Valley, the remnant of a 299-mile line that once reached north to Mound House, Nevada, near Carson City. The museum is located 5 miles northeast of Bishop, California, near the junction of Highway 6 and Silver Canyon Road, in what is left of the old town of Laws. It opened April 1, 1966, 83 years from the day the first scheduled train arrived at Laws from the north; it is operated by the Bishop Museum & Historical So-

ciety. Items of interest include Southern Pacific steam locomotive No. 9, nicknamed *Slim Princess*; freight and passenger cars; the original depot built in 1883; and numerous railroad artifacts and pioneer exhibits.

Although the 11-acre site is accessible to handicapped or people with baby strollers, the grounds are not paved. Guided tours are offered for groups by reservation. Staff is on the premises year-round, and restaurants and lodging are available in Bishop.

Bishop

Locomotives	2 steam, 4 diesel
Cars	Coaches
Displays	Steam and diesel locomotives, freight and passenger cars
Schedule	Weekends and national holidays (except New Year's, Easter, Thanksgiving, and Christmas). Departures from Campo, rain or shine, at 11 a.m., 1 p.m., and 3 p.m. Charter trips available.
Admission	Free
Fares	Adults $7.00. Children 5-12 $3.50 (under 5 free). Fifteen percent discount for groups of 15 or more. Credit cards and checks accepted.
Memberships	Pacific Southwest Railway Museum Association; write to La Mesa address.
Special events	Train ride and barbecue Labor Day and early spring
Nearby attractions	Laguna Mountain recreational area, Cuyamaca Lake, Morena Lake
Address	4695 Nebo Drive (Railroad Avenue), La Mesa, CA 92041
Phone	(619) 478-9937 (Campo); (619) 697-7762 (La Mesa)

PACIFIC SOUTHWEST RAILWAY MUSEUM

The Pacific Southwest Railway Museum Association operates two locations near San Diego. At 4695 Nebo Drive (Railroad Avenue) in La Mesa, visitors can see the original 1894 La Mesa depot — restored by volunteers — as well as an exhibit featuring a steam engine and freight and passenger cars.

The main collection is at the museum in Campo, off Highway 94; road signs will direct you to the museum. Here you can see restoration work in progress, visit the museum store, and ride on the museum's San Diego & Arizona Railway. The 15-mile round trip from Campo to Miller Creek and back takes about 1½ hours. Scenery includes lush meadows, rock cuts and fills, and valleys with live oak groves. Children under 12 riding the train must be accompanied by an adult.

The 8½-acre grounds at Campo are not paved, but are accessible to the handicapped or people with baby strollers. The best time to visit is in early to mid-spring, as temperatures in summer can climb to more than 100°. Restaurants are located in Campo, and lodging is available in Pine Valley and Alpine.

Locomotives	5 steam, 3 diesel
Cars	Open excursion cars
Schedule	Daily, rain or shine, except Christmas Day, with one to five departures depending upon the season
Fares	Adults $9.75. Children 3-15 $6.75. Discounts for groups of 25 or more (reservations required). Credit cards and checks accepted.
Special events	Moonlight steam train
Nearby attractions	Henry Cowell Redwoods State Park
Address	P. O. Box G-1, Felton, CA 95018
Phone	(408) 335-4400, 335-4484

ROARING CAMP & BIG TREES NARROW-GAUGE RAILROAD

This railroad line dates from 1875, when the first narrow-gauge locomotive arrived at Felton. The Roaring Camp & Big Trees has been in operation since 1963. Passenger trains depart from the depot on Graham Hill Road ½ mile southeast of Felton. The depot was built in 1880 by the South Pacific Coast Railroad. Vehicles are banned at Roaring Camp, so visitors walk across a covered bridge and down a country lane to board the train.

The train travels through a redwood forest and up an 8½ percent grade to the top of Bear Mountain. The 6½-mile round trip lasts 1¼ hours. Children must be accompanied by an adult.

A chuckwagon barbecue is served at Roaring Camp weekends, May through October; reservations are recommended. The general store sells gifts, candy, and dry goods, while the Red Caboose Saloon serves hamburgers, hot dogs, soft drinks, and ice cream. A moonlight steam train departs Saturday nights from June through October, and features entertainment, dancing, chuckwagon barbecue, and refreshments; reservations are required.

The grounds are not paved, but assistance is available aboard the train for the handicapped. Lodging is available in Santa Cruz and Scotts Valley. Felton is 80 miles south of San Francisco.

Felton   **CALIFORNIA-9**

Locomotives	2 diesel
Cars	Coaches, combine
Schedule	Daily in spring, summer, and fall. Departures at 11:30 a.m. and 2:30 p.m. Reduced winter schedule.
Fares	Adults $15.00. Children 3-15 $7.50 (under 3 free). Group discounts available. Credit cards and checks accepted.
Nearby attractions	Henry Cowell Redwoods State Park, Santa Cruz beach and boardwalk
Address	P. O. Box G-1, Felton, CA 95018
Phone	(408) 335-4400, 335-4484

SANTA CRUZ, BIG TREES & PACIFIC RAILWAY

This line began operations in the late 1870s as the Santa Cruz & Felton, which was succeeded by the South Pacific Coast. Southern Pacific operated it from 1887 to 1985, when the line was purchased by F. Norman Clark, president and founder of the Roaring Camp & Big Trees Narrow-Gauge Railroad.

Today standard gauge excursion trains run between Roaring Camp and the Pacific Ocean in Santa Cruz. This 14-mile round trip takes approximately 2 hours, with refreshments served aboard the train. Along the way passengers will see redwood forests, the San Lorenzo River gorge, secluded fishing and swimming holes, and, in Santa Cruz, streets lined with Victorian homes. Children must be accompanied by an adult. The grounds are not paved, but assistance is available aboard the train for the handicapped. Restaurants can be found in Felton and Santa Cruz; lodging is available in Santa Cruz.

Locomotives	1 steam, 4 diesel, 2 diesel cars
Cars	Coaches, open observation car
Schedule	Super Skunk service daily, third Saturday in June through second Saturday in September. Diesel car service daily second Sunday in September through third Friday in June, except Thanksgiving, Christmas, and New Year's Day. Departures, rain or shine. Reservations required. Charter trips available.
Fares	Adults $20.00 all-day round trip, $16.00 half-day or one-way trip. Children 5-11 half fare (under 5 free if not occupying a seat). Discounts for groups of 35 or more. Credit cards and checks accepted.
Special events	Steam train specials, wine and barbecue specials
Nearby attractions	Redwoods, botanical gardens, deep-sea fishing
Address	P. O. Box 907, Fort Bragg, CA 95437
Phone	(707) 964-6371

CALIFORNIA WESTERN RAILROAD

The California Western Railroad began in 1885 as a logging line. Steam passenger service started in 1904, was extended to Willits in 1911, and was replaced in 1925 by a Mack railbus nicknamed "Skunk." The nickname came from the smell of the exhaust of the rail car's gasoline engine.

"Super Skunk" passenger trains powered by diesel locomotives make two round trips from Fort Bragg and Willits to Northspur daily during the summer; food and beverages are available at Northspur, the halfway point, where passengers change trains to continue their ride to the other terminal. The 80-mile round trip through the redwoods takes 7½ hours from Fort Bragg and 8½ hours from Willits. The train makes frequent stops to deliver mail and groceries and crosses many bridges and trestles. One-way and half-day trips also are available. Diesel car service is provided daily the rest of the year, except for Thanksgiving, Christmas, and New Year's Day.

Restaurants and lodging are available in Fort Bragg and Willits. The Fort Bragg station is at the foot of Laurel Street; the Willits station is three blocks east of U. S. 101.

Fort Bragg

Locomotives	3 steam
Cars	Coaches, open observation cars
Displays	Steam locomotives, freight and passenger cars, shop and roundhouse facilities
Dates open	Summer weekends. Reservations required for groups.
Admission	Free
Nearby attractions	Columbia State Historic Park
Address	P. O. Box 1250, Jamestown, CA 95327
Phone	(209) 984-3953, 532-0150 (off-season)

P & A 🎁

RAILTOWN 1897 STATE HISTORIC PARK

The Jamestown, Calif., roundhouse, shop, and station facilities of the Sierra Railroad were purchased by the state of California in 1982 and now constitute the Railtown 1897 State Historic Park. The 26-acre park site is located at 5th Avenue and Reservoir Road in Jamestown. The grounds are accessible to handicapped or people with baby strollers. Restaurants and lodging are available in Jamestown.

In addition to viewing the museum displays, visitors can ride excursion trains through rolling foothills and oak woodlands as far as Oakdale — but at press time the state had not been able to find a concessionaire to operate the trains for the 1987 season. It's advisable to check the status, schedules, and fares of the excursion trains with a letter or phone call in advance of your visit.

Displays	Wood caboose, steam locomotive, wood box car, tank car
Dates open	Wednesday through Sunday, 10 a.m. to 5 p.m. Closed Monday, Tuesday, and Christmas Day. Guided tours available by reservation.
Admission	50 cents (infants free)
Special event	Camera day (April)
Nearby attractions	Banning Museum, Coast Botanical Gardens, Marineland, Cabrillo Museum, Maritime Museum, Port of Calls
Address	2135-37 250th Street West, Lomita, CA 90717
Phone	(213) 326-6255

LOMITA RAILROAD MUSEUM

Established in 1966, this city-owned museum reproduces the era of the steam locomotive. It is located on the corner of Woodward Avenue and 250th Street West in Lomita, California. The building, a replica of Boston & Maine's Greenwood Station in Wakefield, Massachusetts, includes an authentically furnished ticket office.

On display are Union Pacific caboose No. 25730; Southern Pacific locomotive No. 1765, a 2-6-0, and tender No. 7334; hand car; and railroad memorabilia such as whistles, marker lights, semaphore signals, number plates, builder's plates, photographs, and drawings.

The grounds also include a park that is ideal for picnics, and a "shower of rainbow" fountain. The museum is accessible to the handicapped. Restaurants and lodging are available in Lomita.

Locomotives	2 diesel powered
Cars	10 open-air Pullman type
Schedule	Daily in summer. Closed Mondays, September-May. Train operates, rain or shine, from 10 a.m. to 4:30 p.m. Charter trips available.
Fares	Adults $1.50. Children 18 months-13 years $1.25 (under 18 months free). Senior citizens age 65 and up $1.00. Group discounts available. Checks accepted.
Special events	Charter trains for picnics
Nearby attractions	Travel Town Railroad, northeast corner of Griffith Park
Address	Railroad Supply Corporation, 115 South Victory Boulevard, Burbank, CA 91502
Phone	(213) 664-6788, 849-1352

GRIFFITH PARK & SOUTHERN RAILROAD

The Griffith Park & Southern Railroad is located just inside the main entrance to Griffith Park, 4400 Crystal Springs Drive, Los Angeles, California. Griffith Park, 4300 acres, is the largest city-owned park in the world; it is at the intersection of Interstate Highways 5 (Golden State Freeway) and 134 (Ventura Freeway).

The 1/3 scale 18½"-gauge trains journey past pony corrals, through an 80-foot-long tunnel, across Lizzard Creek trestle and back through the old Western town of Griffith Gulch to the depot, a reproduction of a nineteenth-century Midwestern station house. The 1¼-mile ride takes about 10 minutes.

The ground are paved and are accessible to handicapped or people with baby strollers. Discounted hotel accommodations in the Burbank area can be arranged with advance notice.

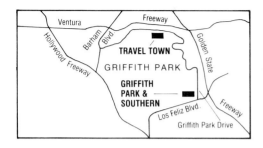

Locomotives	2 diesel
Cars	6 miniature Pullman cars
Displays	Steam locomotives, passenger and freight cars
Schedule	Daily in summer. Weekends and holidays September-May. Train operates, rain or shine, from 10 a.m. to 4:30 p.m. Charter trips available.
Fares	Adults $1.50. Children 18 months-13 years $1.25 (under 18 months free). Senior citizens age 65 and up $1.00. Group discounts available. Checks accepted.
Nearby attractions	Griffith Park & Southern Railroad
Address	Railroad Supply Corporation, 115 South Victory Boulevard, Burbank, CA 91502
Phone	(213) 662-9678, 849-1352

P &. ㅈ ㅍ ▣

TRAVEL TOWN RAILROAD

Travel Town is located at the northeast corner of Griffith Park, near the Forest Lawn entrance. On display there is a collection of full-size locomotives; railroad passenger and freight cars including Pullmans and cabooses; trolleys; old fire trucks and cars; and horse-drawn wagons and buggies. Encircling the museum is the 16″-gauge Travel Town Railroad, which takes visitors past the transportation museum and railroad yard. The 1-mile ride lasts about 10 minutes.

The ground are paved and are accessible to handicapped or people with baby strollers. Discounted hotel accommodations in the Burbank area can be arranged with advance notice.

Los Angeles

Locomotives	1 steam, several diesel and electric
Cars	Streetcars and interurbans
Displays	150 trolleys, interurbans, passenger, freight, and maintenance of way cars, a Ventura County 2-6-2 steam locomotive, and several diesels
Dates open	Weekends and major holidays, 11 a.m.-5 p.m. (until dusk in winter). Daily, December 26-January 1 and the week between Palm Sunday and Easter. Trains operate every 20-30 minutes. Closed Thanksgiving and Christmas Day. Charter trips available.
Admission	Free for grounds and parking except during special events. All-day pass for trolley rides: adults $3.50; children 6-11 $2.00 (under 6 free). Group discounts available (apply in advance). Checks accepted. Memberships available.
Special events	Rail festival last weekend in April, fall festival last weekend in October
Nearby attractions	March Air Force Base museum
Address	P. O. Box 548, Perris, CA 92370-0548
Phone	(714) 657-2605, 943-3020

James W. Walker Jr.

ORANGE EMPIRE TROLLEY MUSEUM

Organized in 1956 by electric rail enthusiasts interested in preserving the remnants of the trolley era, the museum occupies a 53-acre site at 2201 South A Street, about 1 mile south of the center of Perris, California. The 2½-mile round trip trolley ride includes a main line that was part of the original Santa fe route to San Diego, and a loop line through the center of the museum's grounds. The museum's collection includes approximately 150 trolleys, interurbans, passenger, freight, and maintenance of way cars, a Ventura County 2-6-2 steam locomotive, and several diesels.

Children under age 16 must be accompanied by an adult. Restaurants are located in Perris, and lodging is available in Sun City (5 miles) and Riverside (20 miles).

Locomotives	1 steam, 4 diesel
Cars	Caboose and flat cars with benches
Displays	Locomotives, freight, passenger cars
Schedule	Train operates last weekend of month from May through September, plus July 4th and Labor Day weekends. Charter trips available. The museum is open 10 a.m.-5 p.m. — daily, from Memorial Day to the last weekend of September; weekends the rest of the year.
Admission	Free
Fares	$2.00 each, $5.00 for family ticket; good all day. Checks and charge cards accepted. Memberships available.
Special events	National motorized track car championship time trials, first weekend in August
Nearby attractions	Fishing, golfing; Reno, Nevada
Address	P. O. Box 8, Portola, CA 96122
Phone	(916) 832-4131

PORTOLA RAILROAD MUSEUM

The Portola Railroad Museum, operated by the Feather River Rail Society, is housed in the former Western Pacific diesel shop in Portola, approximately 50 miles northwest of Reno, Nevada. A 1-mile train ride around a turning track through the High Sierra pine forest is offered. The museum's collection includes 50 freight cars, 14 locomotives, and 3 passenger cars. The 37-acre grounds are accessible to handicapped or people with baby strollers. Restaurants and lodging are available in Portola.

Portola

Locomotives	1 steam, 4 diesel, 4 electric
Cars	Many streetcars and interurbans
Schedule	Weekends year-round, plus July 4 and Labor Day; noon to 5 p.m. Closed New Year's Day, Thanksgiving weekend, and Christmas. Reservations needed for large groups. Charter trips available.
Admission	Adults through age 64 $3.00, age 65 and over $2.00. Juniors 12-17 $2.00. Children 3-11 $1.00 (under 3 free). Discounts for groups of 40 or more. Checks and charge cards accepted. Memberships available.
Special events	Spring Railway Festival, first weekend in May
Nearby attractions	Marine World, Sacramento River delta
Address	Bay Area Electric Railroad Association, P. O. Box 3694, San Francisco, CA 94119-3694
Phone	(707) 374-2978

WESTERN RAILWAY MUSEUM

Established in 1960, the Western Railway Museum is operated by the Bay Area Electric Railroad Association. It is located on State Highway 12 in California's Solano County, midway between Fairfield and Rio Vista.

Streetcars and interurbans carry visitors on a 1.5-mile track that circles through the grounds and parallels the former Sacramento Northern Railway interurban line. The cars stop near the carbarns, where visitors can observe the museum's members restoring rolling stock. More than 100 pieces of railway equipment — including large collections from the Key System and the Sacramento Northern Railway — are housed at the 25-acre site. Many cars are open for inspection. Steam trains operate on selected weekends.

While the Western Railway Museum's grounds are accessible to handicapped or people with baby strollers, the staff warns that the grounds are not paved. County ordinance prohibits overnight trailer parking. Restaurants and lodging are available in Fairfield and Rio Vista (11 miles), Sacramento and Stockton (45 miles), and San Francisco (55 miles).

Locomotives	Steam
Cars	Coaches, gondolas
Dates open	Museum open daily, 10 a.m. to 5 p.m. Closed New Year's Day, Christmas, and Thanksgiving. Slide show and movie programs on the hour.
Schedule	Excursion trains depart on the hour from 10 to 5 weekends, May through Labor Day (except July 4 weekend).
Admission	Adults $3.00. Children 6-17 $1.00. Discounts for groups of 25 or more adults.
Fares	Adults $3.00. Children 6-17 $2.00 (under 6 free). Charters, special trains, and group rates available.
Nearby attractions	Old Sacramento, state capitol, Old Governor's Mansion, Sutter's Fort, State Indian Museum
Address	111 I Street, Sacramento, CA 95814
Phone	Museum: (916) 445-4209; excursion train: (916) 448-4466

CALIFORNIA STATE RAILROAD MUSEUM

Established in 1981, this museum is located in Old Sacramento State Historic Park, an area of restored and reconstructed buildings from the 1800s containing shops and restaurants. The museum, operated by the California Department of Parks and Recreation, has interpretive and participatory exhibits and includes a roundhouse. The Central Pacific passenger station has been reconstructed to look as it did during the 1870s. Housed in the former Dingley Coffee and Spice Mill, adjacent to the museum's main building, are a gift shop and bookstore.

Twenty-one restored locomotives and cars are exhibited in 100,000 square feet, including Southern Pacific No. 1, *C. P. Huntington*, and cab-forward No. 4294; Central Pacific No. 1, *Governor Stanford*; Virginia & Truckee No. 12, *Genoa*, and No. 13, *Empire*; North Pacific Coast No. 12, *Sonoma*; Georgia Northern private car No. 100, *The Gold Coast*; Canadian National sleeping car *St. Hyacinthe*; and Great Northern postal car No. 42.

Excursion trains run along the banks of the Sacramento River on weekends from May through Labor Day. Trains depart on the hour from the Central Pacific passenger depot near Front and K streets and travel to William Land Park, a 6-mile round trip. Future expansion is planned to Freeport and Hood, 16 miles south of Sacramento.

Streetcars	14
Schedule	Mid-May through mid-October. Departures rain or shine. Charter trips available.
Fares	Adults 75 cents. Children (through age 17) 25 cents. Senior citizens age 65 and over 15 cents. Memberships available in Market Street Railway Company.
Nearby attractions	All of San Francisco
Address	San Francisco Municipal Railway, 949 Presidio Avenue, San Francisco, CA 94115
Phone	(415) 558-2301

SAN FRANCISCO HISTORIC TROLLEY FESTIVAL

The San Francisco Historic Trolley Festival, held from mid-May through mid-October, is sponsored by the city and county of San Francisco in cooperation with the San Francisco Chamber of Commerce. It was first held in 1983 and is the only revenue passenger transit line operating historical streetcars from throughout the world.

The trip begins at the East Bay Terminal, 1st and Mission Streets, then proceeds along Market Street to 17th and Castro, approximately 3 miles. A one-way ride takes approximately 30 minutes.

Other attractions in the area include a cable car turntable at the San Francisco Visitor's Center; cable car barn; and the Historic Trolley maintenance and storage area.

The Market Street Railway Company, 3676 21st Street, San Francisco, CA 94114, is a nonprofit organization devoted to promoting and enhancing San Francisco's vintage streetcar service; the group also sponsors special activities during the festival. Memberships begin at $10.00 per year.

Locomotives	2 steam, 1 gasoline-powered railcar
Cars	15″ gauge gondola and hopper cars, with non-passenger-carrying cars mixed in
Displays	Idle rolling stock when not in use. Full-size cabooses house museum, gift shop, and snack bar.
Schedule	Weekends year-round 11 a.m. to 5 p.m.; daily, summer through Labor Day. Charter trips available.
Fares	Adults $2.20. Senior citizens 65 and up $1.60. Children 16 months-16 years $2.20. Group discounts available.
Nearby attractions	Jack London house, General Vallejo's house, Sebastiani winery, northernmost California mission
Address	P. O. Box 656, Sonoma, CA 95476
Phone	(707) 938-3912

P &. 六 ⛄ ☕ ▄

SONOMA TRAIN TOWN RAILROAD

Train Town is a 10-acre railroad park located on Broadway (Highway 12), 1 mile south of the town square in Sonoma, California. Construction began in 1958 and the railroad has been in operation since 1968. The park includes thousands of trees, lakes, animals, bridges, tunnels, and historic structures. Visitors may take a 1-mile, 20-minute journey aboard a 15″ gauge train. The train passes Lakeville, a 1/4 scale replica of an old-time mining town. Train Town's grounds are paved. Restaurants and lodging are available in Sonoma, approximately 45 minutes north of San Francisco.

Sonoma

Locomotives	5 steam, 1 diesel, 1 gasoline, 1 motor car
Cars	Steel coaches and wood gondolas
Schedule	Not known at press time. Charter trips available.
Fares	Not known at press time. Memberships available.
Special events	July 4 Steam Spectacular, Santa Claus trains
Nearby attractions	Sunol Regional Park, wine country, Great America, Marine World, Africa U. S. A.
Address	P. O. Box 2247, Niles Station, Fremont, CA 94536-0247

P &. A 盒 ■ (⫯)

NILES CANYON SCENIC RAILWAY

The Pacific Locomotive Association was formed in 1961 and began operating the Castro Point Railway in 1969. Its lease for the land containing the museum's storage area was not extended after 1985, so in 1986 the group established the Niles Canyon Scenic Railway. It had not begun operations at press time.

Two routes are expected to be completed during 1987: Sunol to Brightside and back (2 miles each way), and Sunol to Niles and back (6 miles each way). The train will journey through a rustic, winding river canyon. Also planned are maintenance and storage facilities for locomotives and rolling stock. Equipment in the railway's collection includes an 1882 tank locomotive and a 1950 diesel F-unit. The 6-acre grounds are unpaved.

San Francisco is about 45 minutes from the railway. Restaurants and lodging are available in Niles, Pleasanton, and Fremont.

CUMBRES & TOLTEC SCENIC RAILROAD

Please see the listing for Chama, New Mexico.

Locomotives	4 diesel
Cars	10 open cars
Schedule	Railway: April 1 through October. Departures, rain or shine. Museum: May 1 through September. Both open at 8 a.m.
Fares	Adults $3.50. Children 5-11 $2.00. Credit cards accepted. Group discounts available.
Nearby attractions	Rafting, horseback riding, Buckskin Joe (old Western town)
Address	P. O. Box 1387, Canon City, CO 81212
Phone	(303) 275-5485

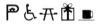

ROYAL GORGE SCENIC RAILWAY

Established in 1957, this 14-inch-gauge railway operates from a depot 1 mile off Highway 50 on Royal Gorge Road, 8 miles west of Canon City, Colorado. The train of open cars runs 1½ miles to the rim of Royal Gorge Canyon at Point Alta Vista, then returns. Royal Gorge Bridge, 1053 feet above the Arkansas River, is the world's highest suspension bridge. Narration is provided during the 30-minute round trip.

Also on the grounds is the Steam Train and Antique Car Museum, which features 3″ scale working steam engines (including an 18,000-pound Mallet) and a diesel switcher. Other displays include 22 steam whistles and mint-condition antique and classic automobiles.

The grounds are accessible to handicapped or people with baby strollers, and free parking is available for cars, campers, and buses. Children must be accompanied by adults; pets are allowed aboard the train. Restaurants and lodging can be found in Canon City.

Antonito   Canon City   **COLORADO-23**

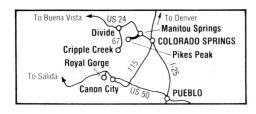

Locomotives	4 steam
Cars	1 closed and 3 open excursion-type cars
Schedule	Daily, Memorial Day weekend through first weekend in October. Departures, rain or shine, every 45 minutes from 10 a.m.
Fares	Adults $4.50. Children 3-12 $2.50 (under 3 free). Group discounts available. Checks accepted.
Special events	Train robberies
Nearby attractions	Palace Hotel with dinner and vaudeville show, Imperial Hotel with dinner and Victorian melodrama, Homestead Parlor House
Address	P. O. Box 459, Cripple Creek, CO 80813
Phone	(303) 689-2640

CRIPPLE CREEK & VICTOR NARROW GAUGE RAILROAD

The Cripple Creek & Victor is located in Cripple Creek, Colorado, a former gold mining town. The 2-foot-gauge steam-powered train departs every 45 minutes from Cripple Creek Museum — the old Midland Terminal Depot — at 5th and Bennett Avenue and carries passengers south out of Cripple Creek past the old Midland Terminal wye, over a reconstructed trestle, and past historic mines, including the deserted mining camp of Anaconda. Stops are made during the 4-mile, 45-minute round trip for interesting scenery and an echo valley. Gun fighters stage a train robbery on alternate weekends.

Restaurants and lodging are available in Cripple Creek or Colorado Springs, 40 miles to the east. Visitors should dress appropriately for Colorado's mountain weather.

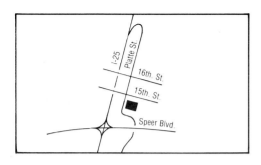

Dates open	Every day except Christmas; 9 a.m. to 5 p.m. Monday through Saturday, 11 a.m. to 5 p.m. Sundays
Admission	Adults $3.00. Age 65 and over $2.70. Children 12-18 $1.50; 5-11 50 cents. Group discounts available. Reservations are required for groups.
Nearby attractions	Children's Museum, Larimer Square (shopping), Union Station
Address	1416 Platte Street, Denver, CO 80202
Phone	(303) 433-3643

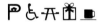

FORNEY TRANSPORTATION MUSEUM

The Forney Transportation Museum was established in 1955 and is housed in the former Denver Tramway Power House, east of Interstate 25 between exits 211 (West 23rd Avenue and Water Street) and 212C (West 32nd Avenue). The museum displays more than 300 transportation items. A 16-minute color movie depicts the history of the area around the museum and spotlights items of special interest.

Among the highlights of the collection are steam locomotives (including Union Pacific "Big Boy" No. 4005), business cars, cabooses, a dining car, four railroad paintings by Denver artist Don Milgrim, and one-of-a-kind automobiles.

The locomotives are outside the museum. While the Forney Transportation Museum is accessible to handicapped or people with baby strollers, there are stairs, and quite a bit of walking is involved.

Locomotives	6 steam
Cars	Coaches, roofed gondola-type cars, snack car, parlor car
Schedule	May 9-October 25, 1987. One to four trains daily, leaving Durango 7:30, 8:30, 9:30, and 10:15 a.m., returning at 3:45, 5:15, 6:15, and 6:55 p.m., plus 4:30 train to Cascade Canyon, returning at 8:45. Reservations required. Charter trips and private cars are available.
Fares	Silverton: adults $28.10; children 5-11 $14.10 (under 5 free if not occupying seat); parlor car $48.30. Cascade Canyon: adults $23.80; children $11.90. Checks accepted; bank-guarantee card required if paying at the station. Parking at Durango: cars $3.50, RVs $4.50.
Nearby attractions	Mesa Verde National Park
Address	479 Main Avenue, Durango, CO 81301
Phone	(303) 247-2733

DURANGO & SILVERTON NARROW GAUGE RAILROAD

The longest-lived portion of the Denver & Rio Grande Western's network of narrow gauge track was a 45-mile line from Durango to Silverton, Colorado. By the early 1950s train service on that line consisted of a mixed freight and passenger train that operated once a week. Then tourists discovered the Silverton train. In the mid-1950s weekend operation began, and by 1964 business had increased to the point that the railroad had to schedule two trains each day and build new passenger cars. In 1968 the Rio Grande abandoned its narrow gauge line from Antonito, Colo., through Durango to Farmington, New Mexico, isolating the Durango-Silverton line.

Charles Bradshaw began negotiations to purchase the Durango-Silverton line in 1979; the sale was completed in 1981 and the opera-

tion was named the Durango-Silverton Narrow Gauge Railroad. The DSNGRR has added locomotives and cars to its roster, and at the height of the summer season Durango now sees five daily train departures. About one-third of the trip is through a broad portion of the valley of the Animas River. At Rockwood the valley narrows to a canyon which the railroad follows, sometimes high above the river and sometimes at water level. The canyon widens just south of the former mining town of Silverton. A layover of 2¼ hours provides ample time to visit the cafes and shops of Silverton before reboarding the train to return to Durango. Overnight layovers are possible in Silverton; trips may begin and end there by using an early-morning bus to Durango.

Cars	1 streetcar
Schedule	Noon to 6 p.m. weekends and holidays, March through October, weather permitting. Charter trips available.
Fares	Adults 75 cents. Children (through age 12) 25 cents. Memberships available in Fort Collins Municipal Railway Society.
Nearby attractions	Rocky Mountain National Park
Address	P. O. Box 635, Fort Collins, CO 80522
Phone	(303) 224-5372

FORT COLLINS MUNICIPAL RAILWAY

Trolleys began operating in Fort Collins in 1907. When service ceased in 1951, the cars were the last Birney cars in scheduled service in North America. The Fort Collins Municipal Railway Society was formed to restore a portion of this trolley system. Volunteers rebuilt almost every piece of wood, glass, and light metal on single-truck Birney car No 21. The car runs on a restored route along West Mountain Avenue from City Park to the edge of the business district. The 3-mile round trip takes 20 to 25 minutes. Restaurants and lodging are available in Fort Collins, approximately 65 miles north of Denver.

Fort Collins   **COLORADO-27**

Locomotives	5 steam, 1 diesel
Cars	Open excursion cars
Schedule	Daily, rain or shine, Memorial Day weekend through Labor Day weekend. Six trips from Silver Plume between 10 a.m. and 4:40 p.m. Five trips from Georgetown between 10:40 a.m. and 4 p.m. Charter trips available.
Fares	Adults $7.50 (plus $2.50 for the optional mine tour). Children 4-15 $3.75 (plus $1.25 for mine tour); under 4 free. Discounts for groups of 20 or more. Credit cards and checks accepted.
Nearby attractions	Loveland Pass, Central City
Address	P. O. Box 217, Georgetown, CO 80444
Phone	(303) 569-2403 (in season), (303) 279-6101 (Denver)

GEORGETOWN LOOP RAILROAD

The Georgetown Loop was opened in 1884 as part of the Colorado Central (later Colorado & Southern) narrow gauge line from Denver and Golden to Silver Plume. The railroad was abandoned in 1939. A three-mile portion of the railroad including the loop and 100-foot-high Devils Gate Bridge was reconstructed in the mid-1970s. The 6-mile round trip takes 70 minutes. Trips start at either Georgetown or Silver Plume, Colorado, approximately 50 miles west of Denver on Interstate 70; take exit 226 for Silver Plume or 228 for Georgetown.

Parking for buses, RVs, and campers is at Silver Plume, as is the gift shop.

The Georgetown Loop Railroad is operated by West/Rail under concession within the Georgetown Loop Historic Mining & Railroad Park, administered by the Colorado Historical Society. Reservations are required for the optional 1-hour guided walking tour of the Lebanon Silver Mine (jackets are recommended). Restaurants and lodging are available in Georgetown.

Dates open	Daily (except major holidays) 9 a.m. to 5 p.m. (to 6 p.m. in June, July, and August).
Admission	Adults $2.50. Age 65 and up $2.00. Children under 16 $1.00. Family ticket for parents and children under 16 $5.50. Group discounts available. Credit cards and checks accepted.
Memberships	Colorado Railroad Historical Foundation — write for information.
Special events	Six three-day weekends of narrow-gauge steam runs; Santa Claus train first weekend in December
Nearby attractions	Buffalo Bill's grave and museum, Coors Brewery, School of Mines Geological Museum
Address	P. O. Box 10, Golden, CO 80402
Phone	(303) 279-4591

COLORADO RAILROAD MUSEUM

The Colorado Railroad Museum is the largest railroad museum in the Rocky Mountains. It is housed in an 1880-style masonry depot at 17155 West 44th Avenue, Golden, at the foot of Table Mountain, 12 miles west of downtown Denver.

Inside the museum are displays of rare old papers, photos, and artifacts relating to railroads that served Colorado and adjoining states. Outside, throughout the 12-acre grounds, are narrow gauge and standard gauge locomotives, cars, trolleys, and other railroadiana from the 1870s to the present. Included are Denver & Rio Grande Western 2-8-0 No. 346, Burlington 4-8-4 No. 5632 and business car 96, Colorado Midland observation car 111, Santa Fe observation car *Navajo*, Fort Collins streetcar No. 22, and three Rio Grande Southern "Galloping Goose" motor cars.

Trains operate six weekends a year, led by No. 346, Colorado's oldest operating narrow gauge steam locomotive. Two Rio Grande Southern Galloping Geese are used on some of these trips. The trains make a 1-mile, 20-minute round trip through the museum's grounds.

The Denver HO Model Railroad Club meets Thursday evenings in the museum's basement, with an operating session the first Thursday of every month; the public is welcome to attend at no charge.

Locomotives	5 steam, 1 diesel
Cars	Open excursion cars
Schedule	Daily, except when raining, Memorial Day to Labor Day. Good-weather weekends in April, May, September, and October. Charter trips available.
Fares	Adults $2.50. Senior citizens age 65 and up and children 5-12 $1.50 (under 5 free). Checks accepted. Group discounts available.
Special events	July 4 celebration
Address	1540 Routt Street, Lakewood, CO 80215
Phone	(303) 232-9262

HIGH COUNTRY RAILROAD

Established in 1972, the High Country Railroad operates from Heritage Square on U. S. Highway 40, Golden, Colorado, 1½ miles west of the junction with U. S. 6. Heritage Square is a 160-acre amusement park and artisans' shopping center.

The 2-foot-gauge High Country Railroad makes a 1½-mile, 15-minute loop around Heritage Square and offers views of Golden and Denver.

Heritage Square has paved grounds, and is accessible to handicapped or people with baby strollers. Several restaurants are located in Heritage Square, and lodging is available in Golden and Denver.

Cars	7 diesel-powered passenger cars
Schedule	Daily, May through October. June-August, eight departures from 8 a.m. to 5:20 p.m. May, September, and October, departures at 9:20 a.m. and 1:20 p.m. Reservations advised.
Display	Steam locomotive No. 5 at Manitou Depot
Fares	Adults $15.00. Children 5-11 $7.00 (under 5 free if held on lap). Group discounts available.
Special events	Occasional steam-up of locomotive No. 4
Nearby attractions	Cheyenne Mountain Zoo, Will Rogers shrine
Address	P. O. Box 1329, Colorado Springs, CO 80901
Phone	(303) 685-5401, (303) 685-1045 (off-season)

MANITOU & PIKES PEAK RAILWAY

The Manitou & Pikes Peak Railway was incorporated in 1888, with financial backing from Zalmon Simmons, of Simmons mattress fame. Operations began June 30, 1891. It is the highest cog railway in the world, and one of only two in North America.

The Swiss-built trains leave from the depot at 535 Ruxton Avenue, Manitou Springs, Colorado, 6 miles west of Colorado Springs, off Highway 24. During the 18-mile round trip the train travels to the summit of Pikes Peak, 14,110 feet above sea level. Here the train makes a sightseeing stop; a gift shop, information desk, and concession counter are located in the Summit House. The round trip takes about 3¼ hours. Because of the thin air at the summit, people with severe cardiac or respiratory problems are advised against riding this train. Minors must be accompanied by an adult. Trains may be canceled in inclement weather, and warm clothing is recommended at all times.

The Manitou & Pike's Peak is accessible to handicapped or people with baby strollers. Staff is on the premises year-round, and restaurants and lodging are available in Manitou Springs and Colorado Springs.

Locomotives	3 diesel
Cars	Coaches
Schedule	Weekends and holidays leave Canaan 1:30 p.m., returning at 4:42 p.m.; there is also a 10 a.m. train returning at 1:12 p.m. during the autumn leaf season and during Canaan Railroad Days. Leave Kent at 10, 12, 2, and 4 for Kent Falls, returning an hour later; leave Kent at 11:10, 1:10, and 3:10 for Hatch Pond, returning 42 minutes later. Weekday charter trips are available.
Fares	Kent-West Cornwall round trip: adults $6, children through age 12 $4, age 62 and over $4. West Cornwall-Cornwall Bridge and trips from Kent: $3 for all passengers. Group discounts are available. Checks accepted.
Special events	Canaan Railroad Days, end of July and beginning of August
Nearby attractions	Mount Riga State Park, other state parks and state forests, Tanglewood (home of the Berkshire Music Festival)
Address	P. O. Box 1146, Canaan, CT 06018
Phone	(203) 824-0339

Scott Hartley

HOUSATONIC RAIL ROAD COMPANY

The Housatonic Rail Road, established in 1983, operates excursion trains over 17 miles of the former Berkshire line of the New Haven Railroad along the Housatonic River between Canaan and Cornwall Bridge, Connecticut. The round trip takes a little over 3 hours. The last regular passenger trains on the route, weekend-only New York-Pittsfield, Massachusetts, trains, were discontinued when Amtrak took over the nation's passenger trains in 1971.

Passengers ride in coaches purchased from Southeastern Pennsyl-vania Transportation Authority; open excursion cars are expected to be in service for the 1987 season. Schedules allow an hour at West Cornwall for sightseeing and meals; passengers may instead remain aboard and continue another 4 miles to Cornwall Bridge. The railroad also operates excursion trains from Kent, Conn., to Kent Falls State Park and to Hatch Pond. Tickets may be purchased at the station or on board. There are restaurants in Canaan; lodging is available in Great Barrington, Mass., 12 miles from Canaan.

Locomotives	2 diesel (ex-New Haven RS3 and U25B)
Cars	Heavyweight coaches
Displays	Approximately 50 locomotives and cars
Dates open	Weekends May-December
Admission	Free (special fare on Railfan Day); donations are accepted
Memberships	Regular, $20 per year; other types available. Benefits include newsletter, training in museum work and operation, passage on Valley Railroad trains.
Special events	Railfan Day, Members' Day
Nearby attractions	Valley Railroad steam train, Shore Line Trolley Museum, Mystic Seaport, New London Submarine Museum, Gillette Castle State Park, Ocean Beach
Address	P. O. Box 97, Essex, CT 06426
Phone	(203) 767-0494

P &. 禾 🎁 ▣

CONNECTICUT VALLEY RAILROAD MUSEUM

The Connecticut Valley Railroad Museum is a nonprofit organization that shares a site with the Valley Railroad at Essex (see next entry), which uses the museum's rolling stock and members to assist its steam-train operation. Once a year the Connecticut Valley Railroad Museum takes over the operation of the Valley Railroad for Railfan Day. The dual organization allows the museum to concentrate on the preservation and display aspects without having to worry about operating a railroad.

The museum has a large collection of locomotives and cars from New England's railroads, including two operating diesels once on the New Haven's roster. The most recent addition is a former Union Pacific E9 repainted in New York Central's "lightning-stripe" paint scheme. The museum is open weekends May through December; guided tours are available. Essex is approximately 30 miles east of New Haven and 40 miles southeast of Hartford on state highways 9 and 153, 4 miles north of the Connecticut Turnpike. Food and lodging are available in Essex and Old Saybrook; lodging is also available in Ivoryton. The grounds are not paved, but they are accessible to the handicapped and people pushing baby strollers.

Locomotives	2 steam, 4 diesel
Cars	Coaches, parlor car
Displays	The collection of the Connecticut Valley Railroad Museum (see previous entry) is on display at Essex.
Schedule	May–October, weekends and holidays, 11:45 a.m., 1:15, 2:45, and 4 p.m. Weekday service and earlier and later trains are added as the weather warms up; trains operate daily from the end of June through Labor Day. Trains operate Wednesday–Sunday in October; Sundays only at 1:15 and 2:45 in November. Trains also operate on a different schedule from the day after Thanksgiving to the last weekend of the year. Boat cruises operate May–October and are not possible with the last trip of the day.
Fares	Train and boat: adults $9.95, children 3-

11 $4.95 (under 3 free); train only: adults $6.95, children 3–11 $2.95; extra fare for parlor car, $1.95; 65 and over 10 percent discount. Checks are accepted. Group discounts are available with advance reservation; charter trips can be operated.

Special events	Mother's Day, Father's Day, Halloween, Christmas trains
Nearby attractions	Valley Railroad steam train, Shore Line Trolley Museum, Mystic Seaport, New London Submarine Museum, Gillette Castle State Park, Ocean Beach
Address	P. O. Box 452, Essex, CT 06426
Phone	(203) 767-0103

The Valley Railroad Company
The Connecticut Valley Line

P & ⛩ 🎁 ▣

VALLEY RAILROAD

In 1968 the New Haven abandoned the southern portion of its rural branch along the Connecticut River from Hartford to Old Saybrook, Conn. The Connecticut Valley Railroad Association, a Hartford-based group which had operated excursion trains over New Haven lines behind a borrowed steam locomotive, was looking for a railroad of its own, and another group of enthusiasts was negotiating to run excursion trains over some portion of the line between Old Saybrook and Middletown. The Valley Railroad was chartered, and the state purchased the track from Penn Central in 1969. The Valley Railroad began operation between Essex and Deep River, 2½ miles, on August 1, 1971. In 1980 the Valley Railroad extended its operations 4 miles south to connect with Amtrak trains at Old Saybrook (ridership did not meet expectations, and the connecting line is now rarely used) and in 1983 service was extended up the river to Chester, 5 miles from Essex.

Valley Railroad trains consist of well-restored, well-maintained coaches and a parlor car, usually pulled by a steam locomotive. The excursion trains connect with boat cruises at Deep River. The train ride takes 55 minutes; the train-and-boat combination takes 2 hours and 10 minutes.

Essex is approximately 30 miles east of New Haven and 40 miles southeast of Hartford on state highways 9 and 153, 4 miles north of the Connecticut Turnpike. Food and lodging are available in Essex and Old Saybrook; lodging is also available in Ivoryton. The grounds are not paved, but they are accessible to the handicapped and people pushing baby strollers.

Cars	Over 25 streetcars and interurbans, including 3 open cars
Dates open	Sundays April-November, plus Saturdays and holidays May-October, plus weekdays Memorial Day-Labor Day, 11 a.m.-5 p.m. Trolleys operate at least every 30 minutes. Charter trips are available.
Admission	Adults $3, children 5-11 $1.50 (under 5 free), 60 and over $2.50. Discounts are available for groups of 15 or more.
Memberships	Branford Electric Railway Association
Special events	National Trolley Festival, October Fall Foliage Special, Rail Fan Day, Santa Claus Special
Nearby attractions	Valley Railroad, Warehouse Point Trolley Museum, Fort Nathan Hale, Yale University
Address	17 River Street, East Haven, CT 06512
Phone	(203) 467-6927

SHORE LINE TROLLEY MUSEUM

The Branford Electric Railway Association was incorporated in 1945 to preserve and operate trolley cars, which were fast disappearing from the American scene. The association purchased a short piece of track in East Haven and Branford, Connecticut, and its first cars moved onto the property from New Haven in March 1947. The museum was opened to the public in 1953, and in 1959 it was given the Sprague Memorial Visitors Center by the family of Frank Julian Sprague, a native of nearby Milford who was considered the father of electric transportation. The museum was placed on the National Register of Historic Places in 1983.

Trolleys operate over 1½ miles of track from East Haven to Short Beach through woodlands and salt marshes and over two major trestles. The round trip, which includes a guided tour of the carbarn, takes about 50 minutes. The museum can be reached from Exit 52 of the Connecticut Turnpike or from U. S. 1. Restaurants and lodging can be found in East Haven, Branford, and New Haven, 4 miles west.

Cars	9 streetcars built between 1902 and 1949
Displays	42 streetcars, rapid transit cars, and electric locomotives, including the first locomotive built by General Electric
Dates open	Memorial Day-Labor Day, Monday-Saturday 10 a.m.-4 p.m., Sundays noon-6; weekends and holidays noon-5 the rest of the year
Admission	Free
Fares	All-day ticket to ride cars: adults $3.75, children 5-15 $2.00, 62 and older $2.75. Checks are accepted with identification. Group discounts are available; reservations are needed for charter trips.
Memberships	Connecticut Electric Railway Association
Special events	Winterfest — the right of way is decorated with lights, and cars operate evenings till 9 mid-December through January 1 except December 24 and December 25
Nearby attractions	Air Museum, Old Newgate Prison, Basketball Hall of Fame, Mark Twain House
Address	P. O. Box 360, East Windsor, CT 06088
Phone	(203) 623-7417

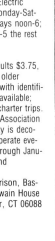

CONNECTICUT TROLLEY MUSEUM

The Connecticut Trolley Museum, operated by the Connecticut Electric Railway Association, Inc., was established in 1940. The first trolley museum in the U. S. to own property, it is located on State Route 140 (North Road) in the Warehouse Point section of East Windsor, on the east bank of the Connecticut River. The museum operates streetcars and interurbans on 1½ miles of former Hartford & Springfield Railway track.

Restaurants and motels can be found nearby and in Hartford and Springfield, Massachusetts, each about 12 miles from the museum.

Locomotives	2 steam, 2 diesel, 1 diesel railcar
Cars	Ex-Lackawanna coaches
Displays	Several steam locomotives
Schedule	Sundays, May-October, noon, 1:15, 2:30, and 3:45. Reservations for special events, caboose rentals, and charters.
Fares	Adults $5, children 2-12 $3 (under 2 free). Checks and credit cards are accepted. Group discounts are available.
Memberships	Historic Red Clay Valley, Inc.
Special events	Theme or reduced fare on most Sundays — mothers ride free on Mother's Day, half fare for senior citizens on Senior Citizen's Day, and so forth. Train robberies are scheduled five times each summer.
Nearby attractions	Longwood Gardens, Winterthur, Hagley Museum, Historic New Castle, Brandywine River Museum
Address	c/o Historic Red Clay Valley, Inc., P. O. Box 5787, Wilmington, DE 19808
Phone	(302) 998-1930; recorded information for groups, (302) 999-9008

WILMINGTON & WESTERN RAILROAD

The Wilmington & Western operates excursion trains over 10 miles of track between Marshallton and Hockessin, Delaware. The line's history goes back to a previous Wilmington & Western Railroad chartered in 1867 and completed in 1872 from Wilmington along Red Clay Creek to Landenberg, Pennsylvania. The road was soon in financial difficulty, and in 1883 it was absorbed by the Baltimore & Ohio, which was building a line from Baltimore to Philadelphia. By the 1960s the line had been cut back to Hockessin and saw a local freight train three days a week.

In 1959 a group of men formed Historic Red Clay Valley, Inc., purchased a Canadian National steam locomotive and some coaches, and reached agreement with B&O to allow operation of steam-powered excursion trains on the branch. Operation began in 1966. In 1982 HCRV purchased the line and in 1984 formed the Wilmington & Western Railway to operate freight service.

Trains operate from Greenbank station, northwest of the intersection of State Routes 2 and 41, about 5 miles west of downtown Wilmington. Trains normally make a 1-hour round trip to the Mt. Cuba Picnic Grove, 5 miles each way; on special occasions trains operate to Hockessin, 10 miles from Greenbank. The Greenbank station area includes a gift shop, snack bar, and museum display. The grounds are not paved, but arrangements can be made to accommodate handicapped persons. There are restaurants nearby on Highway 2; lodging is available in and around Wilmington.

Dates open	Daily except Christmas, 10 a.m.-5:30 p.m.
Admission	Free
Memberships	National Associate program, telephone (202) 357-2700
Nearby attractions	All of Washington
Address	Washington, DC 20560
Phone	(202) 357-2700

SMITHSONIAN INSTITUTION

Railroad Hall of the National Museum of American History, part of the Smithsonian Institution, was opened in January 1964. Exhibits depict the history of American railroads primarily through scale models. There are numerous full-size exhibits, too, dominated by Southern Railway 4-6-2 No. 1401. Other locomotives on display are the Cumberland Valley's *Pioneer* and Camden & Amboy's *John Bull* (recently restored to operating condition).

The museum is located at the corner of 14th Street and Constitution Avenue in Washington, not far from Smithsonian station on the Washington Metro (subway).

38-DISTRICT OF COLUMBIA   Washington

Locomotives	2 steam, 2 diesel
Cars	Coaches (not air-conditioned)
Displays	Freight and passenger cars
Dates open	Daily 10 a.m.-5:30 p.m.
Schedule	Trains operates every half hour weekends and holidays. Charter trips and guided tours are available.
Fares	Adults $4, children 3-11 $2 (under 3 free), 60 and over $3, plus 5 percent state sales tax. Checks accepted. Group discounts available; reservations advisable for groups.
Memberships	Write for information.
Special events	Flagler Day, arts and crafts fair
Nearby attractions	Everglades National Park, Biscayne National Park, MetroZoo, Villa Vizcaya, Miami Seaquarium, Coral Castle, Fairchild Tropical Gardens, Planet Ocean
Address	12450 S. W. 152 Street, Miami, FL 33177-1402
Phone	(305) 253-0063

GOLD COAST RAILROAD MUSEUM

The Gold Coast Railroad was established in 1957 at its present site, but from 1961 to 1985 was located at Fort Lauderdale. It has recently returned to a site adjacent to MetroZoo on Coral Reef Drive (S. W. 152nd Street) just off the Homestead Extension of Florida's Turnpike. The museum grounds are paved and accessible to the handicapped and persons pushing baby strollers. Restaurants and lodging can be found in the nearest town, Cutler Ridge, as well as elsewhere in metropolitan Miami.

The museum operates trains on 1½ miles of track; the 25-minute ride is through pine and palmetto country. The prize exhibit is the Pullman car *Ferdinand Magellan*, which was rebuilt in 1942 for the use of President Franklin D. Roosevelt. Ownership of the car was transferred to the government in 1946. The car was subsequently used extensively by President Truman, very little by President Eisenhower, and on one occasion for campaign purposes by President Reagan. The car has been designated a National Historic Landmark.

The museum's roster of operating locomotives includes two Florida East Coast 4-6-2s, an Atlantic Coast Line SW9, and a Long Island RS3. Steam power is generally used only once a month, either the last weekend or for a special event. The extensive passenger car collection includes a baggage car and a dome observation car from the *California Zephyr*.

Displays	Private car *Rambler*
Dates open	Tuesday-Saturday 10 a.m.-5 p.m., Sunday noon-5, closed Mondays, Christmas, and New Year's Day. Guided tours are offered.
Admission	Adults $3.50, children 6-12 $1.50. Group discounts are available; reservations are required for groups.
Special events	Open house, first Saturday in February
Nearby attractions	Zoo, art museum
Address	P. O. Box 969, Palm Beach, FL 33480
Phone	(305) 655-2833

P & ⊼

HENRY MORRISON FLAGLER MUSEUM

Henry M. Flagler, builder of the Florida East Coast Railway, erected a mansion in Palm Beach for his third wife. The mansion, named Whitehall, was restored in 1960. It is primarily a museum of an opulent life style, but among the exhibits are Florida East Coast memorabilia and Flagler's private car *Rambler*. The museum is located on the east shore of Lake Worth on Cocoanut Row between the Flager Memorial Bridge (Route A1A) and Royal Palm Way (Route 704). Access for the handicapped is limited to the first floor; baby strollers are not permitted.

Locomotives	1 steam, 1 diesel
Cars	Coaches, dining car
Schedule	Saturdays leave Atlanta 10 a.m., noon, 2, and 4 for 18-mile circle or leave Atlanta at 9, noon, and 3 for Stone Mountain Village, returning from Stone Mountain at 10:30, 1:30, and 4:30. Charter trips are operated. Credit cards accepted.
Fares	Adults $10, children 2-12 $5 (under 2 free if not occupying a seat). Discounts for groups of 40 or more.
Nearby attractions	State Capitol
Address	Georgia Building Authority, 1 Martin Luther King Drive, Atlanta, GA 30334
Phone	(404) 656-3253

NEW GEORGIA RAILROAD

The New Georgia Railroad operates trains over two routes, an 18-mile "Zero Milepost Loop" around downtown Atlanta, and from Atlanta to Stone Mountain Village and return, about 16 miles each way. Trains operate from the old Georgia Railroad freight station at 90 Central Avenue, one block north of the state capitol. Motive power is either ex-Southern E8 6901 or ex-Savannah & Atlanta 4-6-2 No. 750. Cars include coaches, a commissary car for snacks and souvenirs, and a dining car. The New Georgia Railroad is operated by the Georgia Building Authority, a state agency, in cooperation with the Atlanta Chapter of the National Railway Historical Society, which owns the locomotives and some of the cars.

Locomotives	Savannah & Atlanta 4-6-2 No. 750 and Southern E8 6901 (usually operating on the New Georgia Railroad in Atlanta)
Cars	2 coaches, baggage car
Displays	Atlanta & West Point 4-6-2 No. 290 (undergoing restoration), numerous industrial locomotives, several cabooses, nearly two dozen passenger cars
Dates open	Weekends except when Atlanta Chapter NRHS is operating excursion trains. Reservations required for guided tours, use of the museum library, and excursion trains.
Schedule	April 18, 19, 25, and 26, October 31, and November 1, 7, and 8 (in cooperation with Norfolk Southern)
Admission	Free; donations are welcomed
Fares	Write for information.
Nearby attractions	Stone Mountain State Park, New Georgia Railroad, Six Flags, High Museum (art)
Address	P. O. Box 13132, Atlanta, GA 30324 (Atlanta Chapter NRHS); 3966 Buford Highway, Duluth, GA 30136 (museum)
Phone	(404) 476-2013

SOUTHEASTERN RAILWAY MUSEUM

The Atlanta Chapter of the National Railway Historical Society operates a museum on a 12-acre site at Duluth, Georgia, about 23 miles northeast of Atlanta. The museum is located at the intersection of U. S. 23 and Berkeley Lake Road; from Interstate 85, use Exit 40, Pleasant Hill Road, north to Duluth, and U. S. 23 south a quarter mile to the museum. Restaurants and lodging can be found in Duluth and nearby Norcross.

Atlanta Chapter NRHS sponsors excursion trains to Toccoa, Ga., and Chattanooga, Tennessee, in cooperation with Norfolk Southern.

Tentative dates for the 1987 season are April 18, 19, 25, and 26, October 31, and November 1, 7, and 8. The trains are usually powered by one of Norfolk Southern's steam locomotives; equipment includes open-window and air-conditioned coaches, an open car, and a snack and souvenir car.

The chapter owns several serviceable steam locomotives and passenger cars, which are usually leased to excursion operators. Savannah & Atlanta 4-6-2 No. 750 operates on the New Georgia Railroad's Zero Milepost Loop around downtown Atlanta (see previous entry).

Locomotives	1 steam, 2 diesel
Cars	2 coaches
Schedule	Steam train operates on principal holidays May–November. Charter trips are operated with either steam or diesel power.
Fares	Adults $5, children through age 12 $3. Checks accepted.
Memberships	Hart County Scenic Railway, $10 and up
Special events	Halloween train, Christmas dinner train
Nearby attractions	Historic Depot Street, Hartwell Lake Dam
Address	P. O. Box 429, Hartwell, GA 30643
Phone	(404) 376-4901

HART COUNTY SCENIC RAILWAY

The Hart County Scenic Railway was established in 1985 as an affiliate of the Hartwell Railway, a short line connecting the town of Hartwell in northeastern Georgia with the Southern Railway at Bowersville. The railway operates on holidays during summer and fall and operates charter trains at nearly any time. Motive power is an ex-Reader Railroad 2-6-2 and a pair of General Electric 44-ton diesels. The two coaches are former Lackawanna electric-powered commuter cars. Refreshments are available on the train. The train runs from the station at 97 Depot Street in Hartwell to Airline, 5½ miles, and back through rolling farmland (there are stretches of 4 percent grade); the round trip takes an hour.

Hartwell is located on Hartwell Lake, which forms part of the Georgia-South Carolina boundary, about 12 miles southeast of I-85. There are restaurants in Hartwell; lodging can be found in Lavonia, 10 miles away, and Anderson, S. C., 20 miles away. The Hart County Scenic Railway is developing facilities that will include a museum.

Displays	Western & Atlantic 4-4-0 *General*, Civil War memorabilia
Dates open	Monday-Saturday, 9:30 a.m.-5:30 p.m.; Sunday, noon-5:30
Admission	Adults $2, children 9-15 $.50, age 65 and over $1. Group discounts available.
Special events	Big Shanty Festival in April
Nearby attractions	Kennesaw Mountain National Battlefield Park, Wildman's Civil War Surplus Shop
Address	2829 Cherokee Street, Kennesaw, GA 30144
Phone	(404) 427-2117

BIG SHANTY MUSEUM

The story of James J. Andrews' raid is one of the best known stories of the Civil War. The locomotive the Union forces seized at Big Shanty, Georgia (now Kennesaw), Western & Atlantic's *General*, is the principal exhibit at the Big Shanty Museum, which opened April 12, 1972, 110 years after Andrews' Raid. Other exhibits tell the story of the raid. The museum is at 2829 Cherokee Street in Kennesaw between U. S. 41 and I-75. Kennesaw is about 25 miles northwest of Atlanta. Food and lodging can be found nearby as well as in Marietta, 9 miles away.

Displays	Steam locomotive, passenger cars, caboose
Dates open	Tuesday-Saturday 10 a.m.-5 p.m., Sunday 2-4. Closed Thanksgiving, Christmas, and New Year's Day.
Admission	Adults $2, children 5-18 $1. Checks accepted. Group discounts available.
Special events	Antique Show (April), Heritage Festival (October), Tour of Homes (December)
Nearby attractions	Okefenokee Swamp Park, Jekyll Island
Address	Route 5, Box 406A, Waycross, GA 31501
Phone	(912) 285-4260

P &♿ 🚅 🎁

OKEFENOKEE HERITAGE CENTER

The Okefenokee Heritage Center traces the history of the region surrounding the Okefenokee Swamp in southeastern Georgia. Railroads are a part of that history, and on display at the museum are a 2-8-2 built by Baldwin in 1912, two baggage cars, a coach, and a caboose. The museum is 3 miles north of Waycross between U. S. 1 and State Route 50. There are restaurants and lodging in Waycross.

Locomotives	2 steam, 1 diesel
Cars	Open coaches
Schedule	Daily except Thanksgiving and Christmas. Trains leave Puukoli at 9:35 a.m., 10:50, 12:05 p.m., 1:50, and 3:05; they stop at Kaanapali 10 minutes later. Trains leave Lahaina at 10:20, 11:35, 1:20, 2:35, and 4:10.
Fares	Adults $7.50 round trip, $4.50 one way; children 12 and under $3.75 RT, $2.25 OW; 65 and over $3.50 RT $2.50 OW. Checks and credit cards are accepted. Tickets may be purchased at stations, at tour and activities desks, or through travel agents. Group discounts available. Reservations necessary for large groups.
Address	P. O. Box 816, Lahaina, HI 96761
Phone	(808) 667-6851; for recorded information 661-0089

LAHAINA KAANAPALI & PACIFIC RAILROAD

Hawaii was served by common-carrier railroads through the 1940s, but after World War Two the trains were replaced by highway transportation — cars and trucks. The last survivor, the Kahului Railroad along the north shore of the island of Maui, was abandoned in 1966, and its rails were used in the construction of the Lahaina Kaanapali & Pacific, which was opened in 1970. The 6-mile, 3-foot-gauge line joins the resort areas of Lahaina and Kaanapali; a round trip on the Sugar Cane Train, as it's known takes 65 minutes. The train travels through fields of sugar cane and along the edge of golf courses and offers views of mountains and the ocean. A double-deck bus provides courtesy transportation between the Lahaina station and the harbor; jitneys connect the station at Kaanapali and the principal hotels. Tour packages that include lunch, boat cruises, and various attractions are available.

Displays	Pioneer Zephyr, Santa Fe 4-8-4 No. 2903, New York Central 4-4-0 No. 999, large model railroad
Dates open	Weekends and holidays 9:30 a.m.-5:30 p.m., Monday-Friday 9:30-4, but 9:30-5:30 daily Memorial Day-Labor Day
Admission	Free, but there are charges for some non-railroad activities and exhibits within the museum.
Memberships	Write for information.
Address	57th Street and Lake Shore Drive, Chicago, IL 60637-2093
Phone	(312) 684-1414

MUSEUM OF SCIENCE AND INDUSTRY

The Museum of Science and Industry, opened in 1933, is the world's largest and most popular museum of contemporary science and technology. Its exhibits include several locomotives, the world's first diesel-electric streamlined train, and a large O scale model railroad. The museum is on Lake Shore Drive (U. S. 41). Parking is free.

Chicago Transit Authority bus routes 1 and 6 (from downtown) and 55 (on 55th Street and Garfield Boulevard) serve the museum. Illinois Central Gulf (Metra) and Chicago South Shore & South Bend trains stop at 57th Street station, about two blocks west of the museum.

Chicago

Locomotives	3 steam, 2 diesel
Cars	Combine, coaches, caboose
Displays	About 50 passenger, freight, and work cars
Schedule	Memorial Day-Labor Day, weekends and holidays; Labor Day-mid-October, Sundays only. Trains leave at 1, 2, 3, and 4 p.m.
Admission	Adults $3, children 6-12 $1.75, age 65 and over $2.25. Price includes train ride. Group discounts available.
Memberships	Write for information.
Special events	World Championship Old-Time Piano Playing Contest (Memorial Day), Father's Day Bluegrass Jam, Railroad Days (September), Ghost Train (Halloween)
Nearby attractions	Robert Allerton Park, Bryant Cottage, Illinois Pioneer Heritage Center
Address	Box 401, Monticello, IL 61856
Phone	(217) 762-9095

MONTICELLO RAILWAY MUSEUM

The Monticello Railway Museum operates trains on a 2-mile stretch of former Illinois Terminal line about halfway between Champaign and Decatur, Ill. The round trip through woods and farmland takes about 40 minutes. At Monticello are a gift shop and several cars containing museum displays. The museum is located on a frontage road at Exit 63 of Interstate 75 just north of Monticello. The museum grounds are not paved, but access is possible for the handicapped and persons with baby strollers. There are restaurants and limited lodging in Monticello; more are available in Champaign and Decatur.

P & ⛐ 🎁 ◨

ILLINOIS RAILWAY MUSEUM

The Illinois Railway Museum is one of North America's largest. It is noted for its collections of diesels, Midwestern interurbans (10 pieces of Illinois Terminal equipment alone), and Chicago streetcars and rapid transit cars. Among the locomotives on display are a GG1, a South Shore "Little Joe," Grand Trunk and Milwaukee Road 4-8-4s, and a Norfolk & Western 2-8-8-2. The museum was established in 1953 in North Chicago and moved in 1964 to its present site on the eastern edge of the village of Union in McHenry County. On the 56-acre grounds are several carbarns, a well-equipped locomotive shop, a station, a bookstore and gift shop housed in a baggage car, and a Chicago "L" station. A loop of track takes streetcars and interurbans around the area; steam and diesel trains operate over 3 miles of track along the roadbed of the former Elgin & Belvidere Electric Railway and parallel to a line of the Chicago & North Western.

The museum is about 50 miles northwest of Chicago. Union is just north of U. S. 20 about halfway between Elgin and Rockford; the museum is on Olson Road ½ mile east of the center of Union. Many of the walkways around the museum and in the carbarns are paved, making access easier for the handicapped and for persons pushing baby strollers. There are restaurants in Union; lodging can be found in Marengo, 3 miles west.

Locomotives	3 steam, 10 diesel
Cars	Heavyweight coaches, complete *Zephyr* train, numerous streetcars and interurbans
Displays	More than 60 interurbans, streetcars, and transit cars, 18 steam locomotives, 18 diesels, 40 passenger cars, plus freight and work equipment
Dates open	Museum is open and electric cars operate Sundays and holidays mid-April through October and Saturdays May-September, 11 a.m.-5 p.m., and Monday-Friday from Memorial Day to Labor Day, 10-4. Steam trains operate weekends and holidays May-September. Charter trips are operated.
Admission	When steam train or *Zephyr* operates: adults $4.50, children 5-11 $2.25; Railfan and Members' Weekends: adults $6.50, children 5-11 $2.25; other times: adults $3.50, children 5-11 $1.50 (children under 5 free). Discounts for senior citizens and groups. Checks and credit cards accepted. Admission price includes rides.
Memberships	Associate membership $15, family $25
Special events	Railroad Day, Chicago Day, Trolley Pageant, Diesel Day, Steam Week, Railfan Weekend (Labor Day weekend), Members' Weekend (last weekend in September)
Nearby attractions	McHenry County Historical Society, Seven Acres Antique Village
Address	Box 431, Union, IL 60180
Phone	(815) 923-4391; for schedules (815) 923-2488 or (312) 262-2266

Union

Locomotives	2 steam, 2 diesel, 1 gasoline
Cars	Coaches with opening windows
Schedule	Weekends and holidays from the first Saturday of May to first Sunday of November, leave Connersville 12:01 p.m. EST, return about 5:30
Fares	Adults $8, children 2-12 $3.50. Checks accepted. Group discounts available. Reservations required for groups.
Memberships	Write for information.
Special events	Special runs for school groups by advance reservation on Wednesdays, Thursdays, and Fridays in May. Christmas runs: last weekend of November and first two weekends of December, leave Connersville 5 p.m. Friday and Saturday, 12:01 p.m. Sunday. Fare $12.50 (all ages). Reservations required.
Nearby attractions	Canal House, former Auburn and Cord auto factories, Mary Gray Bird Sanctuary, Whitewater State Park
Address	P. O. Box 406, Connersville, IN 47331
Phone	(317) 825-2054

Most of Indiana lies in the Eastern time zone, but the northwest and southwest corners are in the Central time zone. Areas near Chicago, Evansville, Louisville, and Cincinnati observe daylight time, but the rest of the state does not observe daylight saving time. To put it another way, since Eastern Standard Time and Central Daylight Time are the same, in summer most of Indiana is on Chicago time.

WHITEWATER VALLEY RAILROAD

In 1865 the Whitewater Valley Railroad was incorporated to build a line from Harrison, Ohio, northwest of Cincinnati, to Hagerstown, Indiana, along the towpath of the Whitewater Valley Canal. The railroad became part of the New York Central System. A new Whitewater Valley Railroad, a tourist railroad, appeared in 1972, and it purchased the line from Penn Central in 1984.

The 16-mile trip from Connersville to Metamora traverses 2 percent grades and offers views of the canal or its remains. A 2-hour layover in Metamora gives time for sightseeing and shopping before the train returns to Connersville. Box lunches are available; they must be ordered at the Connersville station before 11:30 a.m. and will be delivered to the train before departure.

Connersville is about 60 miles from Indianapolis, Cincinnati, and Dayton. The station is on Route 121 (Grand Avenue) about a mile south of the center of Connersville. A gift shop is in the station; various pieces of rolling stock are on display near the station. Restaurants and lodging are available in Connersville; there is a campground half a mile from the station.

Locomotives	2 steam, 5 diesel
Cars	Coaches, combine, snack bar car
Displays	Railway Post Office car, diner, coach, sleeper-lounge car
Schedule	French Lick, West Baden & Southern: weekends and holidays April-November, leave French Lick 10 a.m., 1 p.m., and 4 p.m. EST Springs Valley Electric Railway: daily May-October, weekends in April and November, leave every half hour 10-4
Fares	Adults $6, children 3-11 $3 (under 3 free), age 65 and over $5. Checks and credit cards accepted. Group discounts available. Reservations required for groups.
Memberships	Write for information.
Special events	Train robberies for Muscular Dystrophy Association, last two weekends of August; Dinner on the Diner, first weekend of November
Nearby attractions	French Lick Springs Hotel, Holiday World Amusement Park, Potaka Lake
Address	P. O. Box 150, French Lick, IN 47432
Phone	(812) 936-2405

P ⅍ ⏀ ☕ ▮

INDIANA RAILWAY MUSEUM

The Indiana Railway Museum was established in 1961 and operated in Westport then in Greensburg before acquiring 16 miles of Southern Railway track between French Lick and Dubois in 1978. In 1980 the museum was given 2 miles of the former Monon branch to French Lick by the Sheraton Hotel Corporation. The museum's steam train operation is known as the French Lick, West Baden & Southern Railway. It runs from French Lick to Cuzco, 10 miles, through part of the Hoosier National Forest and through one of Indiana's longest railroad tunnels. The round trip takes 1 hour 45 minutes. The train carries a snack bar car. The museum also operates a streetcar between French Lick and West Baden (1 mile) as the Springs Valley Electric Railway. Both depart from the former Monon passenger station, which is owned by the French Lick Springs Hotel. It is right at the junction of Routes 145 and 56 in French Lick. French Lick, which is two hours from Indianapolis and an hour from Louisville, offers a variety of hotels and restaurants.

French Lick

Locomotives	4 steam
Cars	Open cars
Displays	Steam-powered machinery
Dates open	Weekends and holidays Memorial Day-Labor Day, then Sundays only through October: noon-5 p.m. CDT. Train operation depends on weather and track conditions. Charter trips can be arranged.
Admission	Free, except during Civil War Reenactment and Hesston Steam & Power Show: adults $2, children 12 and under free
Fares	Adults $2, children 12 and under free
Memberships	$10 annually, $30 for families
Special events	Whistle-stop Days (opening weekend), Civil War Reenactment, Hesston Steam & Power Show, Cider Fest
Nearby attractions	Lake Michigan, Indiana Dunes State Park, Washington Park Zoo in Michigan City, Lighthouse Museum
Address	LaPorte County Historical Steam Society, 2940 Mount Claire Way, Long Beach, Michigan City, IN 46360
Phone	(219) 872-7405 (LaPorte County Historical Steam Society), 872-5055 (LaPorte County Tourism)

Ⓟ ♿ ⛩ ☕ ◧

HESSTON STEAM MUSEUM

In 1957 the LaPorte County Threshermen established a museum of traction engines and other steam-powered machinery at Hesston, east of Michigan City on the Indiana-Michigan border. A steam locomotive was added to the collection in 1964. Subsequently the museum grew through the generosity of Elliott Donnelley. A fire on May 25, 1985, destroyed nine 2-foot-gauge and 3-foot-gauge cars and severely damaged several locomotives. One locomotive, a 2-foot-gauge 0-4-0T from the Darjeeling & Himalayan Railway in India, thought to be irrepairable, has already been restored; other locomotives are under restoration.

Trains of four track gauges circle the museum site. A 2½-mile loop of dual gauge track carries 2-foot-gauge and 3-foot-gauge trains, and there are separate 1-mile loops of 14-inch and 7½-inch-gauge track.

Hesston appears on few maps. To reach the museum, use Michigan Exit 1 of I-94, go south on Indiana Route 39 to County Road 1000 North just south of the state line, then east about 2½ miles to the museum. There are restaurants in Hesston; lodging can be found in LaPorte, 12 miles south; Michigan City, 15 miles west; and New Buffalo, Mich., 6 miles northwest.

Locomotives	1 steam, 2 diesel, 2 electric
Cars	Interurban cars and heavyweight and stainless steel coaches, some air-conditioned
Displays	Approximately 70 cars and locomotives
Dates open	Weekends and holidays April-November noon-5 p.m. Guided tours daily April-November by advance arrangement.
Fares	Adults $2.50, children 6-12 $2. Checks accepted. Group discounts available. Reservations required for groups.
Memberships	Write for information.
Special events	Fairtrain to Indiana State Fair (August)
Nearby attractions	Conner Prairie Settlement, Indianapolis Zoo, Indianapolis Union Station
Address	Box 83, Noblesville, IN 46060
Phone	(317) 773-6000

TRAINS: J. David Ingles

INDIANA TRANSPORTATION MUSEUM

The Indiana Transportation Museum is located in Forest Park in Noblesville, about 20 miles north of Indianapolis on Route 19. Trains operate over a mile of track along the edge of the park; the ride takes about 15 minutes. The museum's operating locomotives include two electrics, Nickel Plate 2-8-2 No. 587, and a pair of former Milwaukee Road F7 diesels. The grounds are partially accessible to the handicapped. Visitors can find restaurants in Noblesville and lodging in Indianapolis.

Noblesville

Locomotives	1 steam, 1 diesel
Cars	Coaches, open cars, caboose
Schedule	Sundays and holidays Memorial Day to mid-October, also Saturdays mid-June to Labor Day: leave Pleasant Lake 1 and 2 p.m. EST. Charter trips operated.
Fares	Adults $3.50, children 5-11 $2 (under 5 free). Checks accepted. Discounts available for groups of 20 or more.
Memberships	Write for information.
Special events	Fathers' Day, 101 Lakes Festival, Firecracker Special (July 4), Pleasant Lake Day, fall train robbery, fall color runs
Nearby attractions	Indiana lake country
Address	P. O. Box 178, Angola, IN 46703
Phone	(219) 825-9182, 833-1804

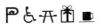

LITTLE RIVER RAILROAD

The world's smallest standard gauge Pacific-type steam locomotive is the feature attraction of the Little River Railroad. The engine was built by Baldwin in 1911 for a previous Little River Railroad which ran through the Smoky Mountains of eastern Tennessee. The locomotive now hauls passengers over 3 miles of former New York Central track in the northeast corner of Indiana. Trains depart from Pleasant Lake, 4½ miles south of Angola (Exit 148 off Interstate 69), and run south to Steubenville and then return. There are restaurants and motels in Angola.

Locomotives	2 diesel
Cars	Ex-South Shore coaches and converted box cars
Displays	Approximately 20 locomotives and cars
Schedule	Memorial Day weekend through October: weekends and holidays, 11 a.m. and 1, 3, and 5 p.m.; Monday-Friday 11 a.m., also Monday-Friday, 1 p.m. during October. Charter trips operated by reservation.
Fares	Adults $7, children 5-15 $3. Checks accepted.
Memberships	Write for information.
Special events	Pufferbilly Days the weekend after Labor Day
Nearby attractions	Mamie Eisenhower Birthplace and Museum, Ledges State Park, Kate Shelley High Bridge, Kate Shelley Memorial Park and Railroad Museum in nearby Moingona
Address	P. O. Box 603, Boone IA 50036
Phone	(515) 432-4249

Paul K. Swanson

BOONE & SCENIC VALLEY RAILROAD

The Fort Dodge, Des Moines & Southern Railroad, an interurban line between Des Moines and Fort Dodge, Iowa, was noted for a high trestle over Bass Point Creek near Boone. In 1971 the Chicago & North Western leased the FDDM&S and in 1983 abandoned most of it. The Boone Railroad Historical Society purchased 11 miles of the line from Boone to Wolf Crossing, including the high bridge, and formed the Boone & Scenic Valley Railroad to operate excursion trains over the line. Diesel-powered trains depart from a station at 11th and Division Streets in Boone and operate over 6 miles of track. The round trip takes 1 hour and 25 minutes. The highlight of the trip is the 156-foot-high bridge. The train offers views of the Des Moines River valley.

Boone is in central Iowa, 42 miles north-northwest of Des Moines and 15 miles west of Ames. To reach the station from U. S. 30, take Story Street north through the business district, turn left on Tenth, and drive 6 blocks west. Food and lodging can be found in Boone.

Cars	2 interurbans, 2 streetcars, 2 open cars
Schedule	Operates only during the Midwest Old Threshers Annual Reunion, a five-day event ending on Labor Day, 6 a.m.-midnight
Admission	Old Threshers Reunion, $5, good for all five days (children under 10 free)
Fares	Round trip 75 cents, one way 40 cents, 10-ride ticket, $2.50. Children under 6 free.
Memberships	Write for information.
Address	P. O. Box 93, Mt. Pleasant, IA 52641

P ♿ ☂ 🎁 ☕ 🍴

MIDWEST ELECTRIC RAILWAY

The Midwest Old Threshers Reunion is an annual event held for five days ending on Labor Day. It is a combination of a fair, antique agricultural equipment show, farm life museum, and campout. The Midwest Electric Railway operates a 1½-mile loop of track connecting the campground with the exhibition areas; also on the grounds is a narrow-gauge steam railroad. Mt. Pleasant is 25 miles west of Burlington on U. S. 34. In addition to the campground of the Old Threshers Reunion there are restaurants and a few motels in Mt. Pleasant; lodging may be easier to find in Burlington and Keokuk.

**KENTUCKY
RAILWAY
MUSEUM**

Locomotives	1 steam, 3 diesel
Cars	Coaches, some air-conditioned
Displays	Approximately 75 locomotives and cars
Dates open	May, September, October: Saturdays and holidays 11 a.m.-5 p.m., Sundays 12:30-5:30; June-August: Tuesday-Saturday 11-5, Sunday 12:30-5:30 (closed Monday)
Schedule	Write for information on mainline excursions.
Admission	Adults $2, children 6-12 $1.50 (children 5 and under free), age 65 and over $1.50. Checks and credit cards accepted. Group discounts available.
Memberships	Associate membership $15, active membership $25; write for information on other categories.
Address	P. O. Box 22764, Louisville, KY 40222-0764
Phone	(502) 245-6035

KENTUCKY RAILWAY MUSEUM

The Kentucky Railway Museum opened in 1954 on River Road in Louisville. A 1964 flood prompted a search for a new location on higher ground, and in 1977 the museum moved to its present location at LaGrange Road (Route 146) and Dorsey Lane in suburban Jefferson County east of Louisville. The collection includes Louisville & Nashville 152, a 4-6-2 built in 1905 by Rogers, and Monon BL2 No. 32, both of which have been restored and are used on mainline excursions. There is an extensive collection of passenger cars. The museum operates trains on a half mile of track at the museum and also operates mainline excursion trains in cooperation with Seaboard System.

Louisville

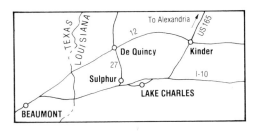

Displays	Southern Pacific 0-6-0 124, Amtrak coach, Missouri Pacific caboose, 2 tank cars
Dates open	Year-round Wednesday-Sunday, noon-4 p.m.
Admission	Free; donations accepted
Memberships	Individual $2.50, families $5
Special events	DeQuincy Railroad Days (second weekend in April)
Nearby attractions	All Saints Episcopal Church, Dog Trot Museum, Sabine National Wildlife Refuge
Address	P. O. Box 997, DeQuincy, LA 70633
Phone	(318) 786-2823

℗ ♿ 🌲

DeQUINCY RAILROAD MUSEUM

The city of DeQuincy, Louisiana, got its start as a railroad town — it is the junction of Kansas City Southern's main line from Kansas City to Port Arthur, Texas, with a 23-mile branch to Lake Charles, La., and also with a Union Pacific (ex-Missouri Pacific) line from New Orleans. The museum was established in 1976; a year previously in response to a request from a federation of women's clubs the KCS had donated its station building and grounds to the city for a park. On display in the museum are photos, models, hardware, and other railroad memorabilia. DeQuincy is about 50 miles northeast of Beaumont, Texas, at the junction of Louisiana Routes 12 and 27. The museum is in downtown DeQuincy on Lake Charles Avenue. The 5-acre museum grounds include playground equipment for children. Restaurants and lodging are available in DeQuincy and in nearby Lake Charles.

Displays	Southern Pacific 2-8-2 745, compressed-air locomotive, passenger and work cars, collection of dining car china and silver
Dates open	Year-round Tuesday-Friday 9 a.m.-4 p.m., Saturday 9-5, Sunday 1-5. Closed on federal holidays.
Admission	Adults $1, children 12 and under 50 cents. Checks accepted. Group discount available by advance arrangement.
Memberships	$15 per year
Special events	Old Kenner Railway Association Festival (May)
Nearby attractions	Kenner City Museum, Louisiana Wildlife and Fisheries Museum, New Orleans
Address	P. O. Box 1835, Kenner, LA 70063
Phone	(504) 468-7223

LOUISIANA STATE RAILROAD MUSEUM

The Louisiana State Railroad Museum was established in 1984 by the Old Kenner Railway Association, which is affiliated with the Pontchartrain Chapter of the National Railway Historical Society. The museum is at 519 Williams Boulevard in Kenner, between U. S. 61 (Airline Highway) and the Mississippi River, half a mile from New Orleans International Airport and right next to the Kansas City Southern and Illinois Central Gulf line. Inside are photos, memorabilia, a collection of dining car china and silver, 9″-gauge and 15″-gauge live steam locomotives, an operating N scale model railroad, HO and O scale model railroads under construction, and various hands-on exhibits. Displays outside include a Southern Pacific 2-8-2, small electric, diesel, and compressed-air locomotives, a coach, a caboose, and a complete wrecker train. There are numerous hotels, motels, and restaurants near the museum.

Locomotives	3 steam
Cars	Coach, open car, caboose
Displays	Antique autos
Dates open	Daily 9:30 a.m.-5 p.m. mid-June to mid-September; also weekends through Columbus Day
Schedule	Train operates every half hour.
Admission	Adults $4, children 12 and under $2. Checks and credit cards accepted. Group discounts available.
Memberships	Individuals $15, families $25
Special events	Father's Day, Antique Engine Meet, Antique Auto Days, Great Train Robbery, Children's Day
Nearby attractions	Boothbay Playhouse Theatre Museum, Grand Banks Schooner Museum, Fort Edgecomb, Lincoln County Jail and Museum
Address	Box 123, Boothbay, ME 04537
Phone	(207) 633-4727

Bob Hayden

BOOTHBAY RAILWAY VILLAGE

In most of the U. S. "narrow gauge" meant rails 3 feet apart. In Maine it was a foot less. The last two decades of the nineteenth century saw a number of 2-foot-gauge railroads built into rural Maine. Boothbay Railway Village, established in 1965, re-creates the atmosphere of turn-of-the-century Maine, with a 1½-mile circle of 2-foot-gauge track around a recreated rural hamlet. The train ride takes about 15 minutes; the trains are powered by German-built four-wheel tank engines (a tank engine carries its water in tanks placed over or alongside the boiler and its fuel in a bunker behind the cab instead of in a separate car, a tender, behind the locomotive). Access to the 8-acre museum grounds is somewhat limited for the handicapped or those pushing a stroller. The museum is on Route 27 in Boothbay, 10 miles south of Wiscasset; Wiscasset is about 50 miles east of Portland. Staff members are on the premises year-round. Restaurants and lodging are available in nearby Boothbay Harbor.

SEASHORE TROLLEY MUSEUM

The Seashore Trolley Museum began with the preservation of an open car of the Biddeford & Saco Railway in 1939. It now encompasses the largest and most diverse collection of electric railway equipment in the country. The more than three dozen streetcars, rapid transit cars, and work cars from Boston include members of most of Boston's PCC classes. Among the foreign cities represented are Berlin, Glasgow, Hamburg, Liverpool, Nagasaki, and Sydney. Cars operate over a mile of track that was once part of the Atlantic Shore Line Railway, and shuttle cars link the main building of the museum with the exhibit barns.

The museum is operated by the New England Railway Historical Society. It is located about halfway between Portsmouth, New Hampshire, and Portland, Maine. To reach the museum from the south and west, take the Maine Turnpike north to Exit 3, then Route 35 east into Kennebunk. Turn left (north) on U. S. 1. At the flashing yellow signal 2.8 miles north of Kennebunk, turn right (east) onto Log Cabin Road and drive 1.7 miles to the museum. From Kennebunkport take North Street from the west end of Maine Street; it's 3.2 miles to the museum. Staff is on the premises year-round. Lodging and restaurants can be found in Kennebunkport, a summer resort area.

P &. 开 î

Cars	Streetcars, open cars, interurbans, and rapid transit cars
Displays	More than 90 electric passenger cars of all types, plus work equipment and freight cars
Dates open	Daily mid-June through Labor Day, 10 a.m.-5:30 p.m., week after Labor Day, noon-5. Weekends Memorial Day to mid-June and Labor Day through October, noon-5. Weekdays late April to mid-June and mid-September to mid-October, enter at 1:30 p.m. for 2-hour guided tour and rides.
Schedule	Rides every half hour spring and fall weekends and daily in summer. Charter trips available.
Admission	Adults $3.50, children 6-16 $2 (children under 6 free), $11 maximum per family, age 60 and over $3. Friday evening trolley ride (July and August) $1, two rides for $1.25. Different charges apply for some special events. Group rates available. Checks and credit cards accepted. Write for information.
Memberships	
Special events	One or two Sundays a month are theme days, when the museum operates a particular type of car: city, Canadian, interurban, and so forth.
Nearby attractions	Beaches, Wedding Cake House, Brick Store Museum
Address	P. O. Drawer A, Kennebunkport, ME 04046
Phone	(207) 967-2712

Displays	Replicas of B&O's earliest locomotives and cars, Camelback and Shay locomotives, early diesels, wide range of steam locomotives, exhibits showing development of track, signals, and bridges, HO scale model railroad
Dates open	Wednesday-Sunday, 10 a.m.-4 p.m. Closed major holidays.
Admission	Adults $2.50, children 6-12 $1.50, age 65 and over $1.50
Nearby attractions	Baltimore Streetcar Museum, Fort McHenry, Harbor Place, Ellicott City B&O Railroad Station Museum
Address	901 West Pratt Street, Baltimore, MD 21223
Phone	(301) 237-2387

B&O RAILROAD MUSEUM

The Baltimore & Ohio Railroad, now part of CSX, was the first common carrier railroad in the U. S. and the first to offer scheduled freight and passenger service. The museum was established in 1953 by the historically conscious B&O, and at that time its collection covered the B&O's history from a replica of the *Tom Thumb* of 1829 to a recently retired passenger diesel. The collection soon included items from other railroads, and it kept expanding. The chief building of the museum is a full-circle roundhouse that was part of B&O's Mount Clare shop complex; the entrance to the museum is through the former Mount Clare station, which was the first railroad station in the U. S. The B&O Museum is on Pratt Street in Baltimore. Access is easiest from the southwest: Frederick Road and U. S. 1 intersect Pratt Street about a mile west of the museum, and Washington Boulevard aims right at the museum.

Cars	11 streetcars
Dates open	Sunday year-round noon-5 p.m.; June-August, Thursday 7-9 p.m. and Saturday noon-5. Groups can be accommodated at any time, but reservations 3 weeks in advance are necessary. Groups planning to visit during regular hours should notify the museum 2 weeks ahead.
Admission	Free
Fares	Adults $1, children 4-11 50 cents, all-day pass $3. Checks accepted. Groups are given two rides for a single fare.
Memberships	Write for information.
Nearby attractions	B&O Railroad Museum, Fort McHenry, Ellicott City B&O Railroad Station Museum
Address	P. O. Box 4881, Baltimore, MD 21211
Phone	(301) 547-0264

BALTIMORE STREETCAR MUSEUM

Three blocks northwest of the Amtrak station in Baltimore at 1901 Falls Road is the Baltimore Streetcar Museum. Its collection is limited to streetcars used in Baltimore because of a unique track gauge, 5′4½″. Cars operate on ⅝ mile of track along Falls Road past the former Maryland & Pennsylvania Railroad roundhouse and freight station. In addition to the streetcars (2 horse-drawn and 11 electric) there is an audiovisual presentation titled *Rails Into Yesterday* depicting the history of street rail transportation in Baltimore. To reach the museum by car, take the North Avenue exit from the Jones Falls Expressway (I-83), go east over the viaduct to Maryland Avenue, turn right (south), and at the next corner, Lafayette Avenue, turn right again, and then take a third right onto Falls Road.

Displays	Chesapeake Beach Railway memorabilia
Dates open	Spring, summer, and fall, Saturdays and Sundays 1-4 p.m.; June-August 1-4 daily
Admission	Free
Memberships	$5 annually
Special events	Antique Auto Show third Sunday in May, Christmas Open House first Sunday in December
Nearby attractions	Battle Creek Cypress Swamp, Calvert Marine Museum
Address	P. O. Box 783, Chesapeake Beach, MD 20732
Phone	(301) 257-3892; 855-6472 for recorded information

CHESAPEAKE BEACH RAILWAY MUSEUM

The Chesapeake Beach Railway was opened in 1900 from Seat Pleasant, Maryland, on the District of Columbia border, to Chesapeake Beach, a resort 28 miles southeast on the shore of Chesapeake Bay. Among its backers were two Colorado railroad builders, Otto Mears and David Moffat. The line was abandoned in 1935, having succumbed to the competion of automobiles on paved highways. The road's one surviving station at Chesapeake Beach was offered to the Calvert County Historical Society in 1979, and the sole remaining Chesapeake Beach passenger car, a coach named *Dolores*, was brought to the station. The museum contains pictures and artifacts of the Chesapeake Beach Railway. Chesapeake Beach is southeast of Washington and south of Annapolis on Maryland Routes 260 and 261. The museum is at 21st and C Streets. There is a restaurant next to the museum, and lodging can be found in nearby North Beach and Rose Haven.

Displays	Restored caboose (can be rented for birthday parties), model railroad depicting B&O's early days, archeological dig at turntable site
Dates open	January-March, Saturday 11 a.m.-4 p.m. and Sunday noon-5; April-December, Wednesday-Saturday 11-4 and Sunday noon-5. Closed major holidays.
Admission	Adults $2, children 5-12 $1, age 62 and over $1.50. Checks and credit cards accepted. Discount for groups of 20 or more.
Special events	Christmas in July (July 15-19 and 22-26), Haunted Station (October 28-31), Treasury of Trains (November 14, 15, 19-22, and 27-29), Old Fashioned Christmas Gardens (December 19, 20, 23, 24, 26, 27, 30, 31 and January 2, 3, 6-10, 1988)
Nearby attractions	B&O Railroad Museum, Baltimore
Address	P. O. Box 244, Ellicott City, MD 21043
Phone	(301) 461-1944

MODEL RAILROADER: Gordon Odegard

ELLICOTT CITY B&O RAILROAD STATION MUSEUM

The first terminus of the Baltimore & Ohio Railroad was Ellicott City, 13 miles from Baltimore. The station at Ellicott City has become a museum, a cooperative project of Howard County and Historic Ellicott City, Inc. In addition to the exhibits and displays, the main station building houses a library and a gift shop. The freight house contains an HO scale model railroad depicting the early B&O.

Between the two buildings the turntable area is being excavated by archeologists. The museum is at the corner of Maryland Avenue and Main Street in Ellicott City. Restaurants and antique and specialty shops are nearby. Lodging can be found in Columbia, 5 miles away, and throughout metropolitan Baltimore.

Ellicott City

Locomotives	10 diesel
Cars	Streamlined coaches, dome diner, open-window coach, gondola
Displays	Western Maryland Railway Historical Society museum
Schedule	Generally, trains operate the first and third weekends of the month, June-November, and most depart from Union Bridge at 1 p.m. Charter trips are available.
Fares	Union Bridge to Keymar and Linwood, adults $5, children 12 and under $3; Union Bridge to Walkersville and Taneytown, $10/$5; Union Bridge to Highfield, $15/$8; Westminster to Highfield, $20/$10. Age 60 and over 10 percent discount. Discounts for groups of 20 or more. Checks accepted.
Special events	Taneytown Fair Day, Westminster Railfest, Union Bridge Volunteer Fire Department Day, Thurmont Catoctin Colorfest, Autumn Gold Special
Nearby attractions	Catoctin Mountain Park, Gettysburg National Military Park, Monocacy Battlefield
Address	P. O. Box A, Union Bridge, MD 21791
Phone	(301) 775-2520

MARYLAND MIDLAND RAILWAY

The Maryland Midland was established in 1980 to operate the Taneytown-Walkersville portion of the former Pennsylvania Railroad branch from York, Pennsylvania, to Frederick, Maryland. In 1983 the road acquired the former Western Maryland main line from Westminster to Highfield, Md. The railroad runs four different diesel-powered round-trip excursions: *Blue Mountain Limited* (Union Bridge-Highfield, 50 miles, 4 hours, and occasionally Westminster-Highfield, 75 miles, 6 hours), *Sunday Local* (Union Bridge-Keymar-Linwood, 10 miles, 1 hour), and *Monocacy Valley Flyer* (Union Bridge-Walkersville-Taneytown, 40 miles, 4 hours). *Blue Mountain*

Limited and *Monocacy Valley Flyer* trips depart Union Bridge at 1 p.m. (Westminster at noon), and *Sunday Locals* depart Union Bridge (41 North Main Street) at 2. Special excursions are operated several times a year from other towns along the line. Snacks and souvenirs are available on the train. Handicapped persons can be accommodated with advance notice. Union Bridge is between Frederick and Westminster on Maryland Route 75; it is about 40 miles northwest of Baltimore. Food and lodging can be found in Westminster, Frederick, and Thurmont.

Cars	14 streetcars
Dates open	Year-round (except December 15-January 1), weekends noon-5 p.m.; also Memorial Day, July 4, and Labor Day, noon-5, and Wednesdays in July and August, noon-4
Admission	Free
Fares	Adults $1, children under 18 75 cents (under 2 free). Checks accepted.
Memberships	Write for information.
Special events	Parade of Trolleys, third Sundays of April and September
Nearby attractions	Washington, D. C.
Address	P. O. Box 4007, Colesville Branch, Silver Spring, MD 20904
Phone	(301) 384-9797

NATIONAL CAPITAL TROLLEY MUSEUM

Streetcar service ended in Washington, D. C., on January 28, 1962, and the cars were sent off to second careers in Texas, Spain, and Yugoslavia. By then the National Capital Trolley Museum had been established, and within a decade it was operating cars and building a collection that included a number of cars from Europe. The museum's visitors' center houses exhibits depicting the history of Washington's streetcar system. Streetcars make a 1¾-mile, 20-minute round trip. The museum is located in Northwest Branch Regional Park at 1313 Bonifant Road, between Layhill Road (Maryland Route 182) and New Hampshire Avenue (Route 650) — or 14 miles due north of the White House. Food and lodging can be found in Wheaton and throughout the metropolitan area.

Locomotives	1 diesel
Cars	3 ex-Lackawanna coaches
Fares	$2, all ages. Group discounts available.
Memberships	Write for information.
Nearby attractions	Basketball Hall of Fame, Volleyball Hall of Fame
Address	P. O. Box 711, Holyoke, MA 01041
Phone	(413) 536-1646

P & 木

Scott Hartley

HOLYOKE HERITAGE PARK RAILROAD

The Pioneer Valley Railroad, a short line running from Westfield to Holyoke and Northampton, Massachusetts, and the Holyoke Heritage Park Railroad team up to operate tourist trains from the Holyoke Heritage State Park to a shopping mall a couple of miles away. Pioneer Valley provides the rails and the locomotive, and Holyoke Heritage Park Railroad provides the passenger cars. Operation of this line was suspended in the spring of 1986 when the railroad's insurance company withdrew its coverage. Operation will resume when insurance can be arranged.

Locomotives	3 diesel
Cars	Coaches, cafe and lounge cars, parlor cars
Schedule	Mid-June to mid-October: Leave Braintree 10:15 a.m., 1:15 p.m., and 7:00 p.m. Monday-Friday; 10:15 a.m. and 8:00 p.m. Saturday; 11 a.m. and 8 p.m. Sunday. Leave Hyannis 7:30 a.m., 10:30 a.m., and 4:30 p.m. Monday-Friday; 7:30 a.m. and 5:30 p.m. Saturday; 8:30 a.m. and 5:30 p.m. Sunday. Write for information on intermediate times and short excursions. Chartered cars and trains operated.
Fares	Braintree to all stations between Buzzards Bay and Hyannis: one way, adults $7, children 4-11 $3.50 (under 4 free); double for round trip. Parlor car supplement $4 one way, $6 round trip. Lower fares apply to intermediate points; special fares apply to excursion packages. Age 62 and over, $1 off on afternoon

Kalmbach Publishing Co.: George Drury

excursions. Group discounts available. Checks accepted.

Nearby attractions	Cape Cod, Boston, Plymouth
Address	252 Main Street, Hyannis, MA 02601
Phone	(617) 771-1145 (information); 771-7008 (business)

CAPE COD & HYANNIS RAILROAD

Passenger train service between Boston and Cape Cod was discontinued in 1959 by the New Haven. A new expressway from Boston through Plymouth to The Cape promised the speed, comfort, and convenience of your own car — and soon, monumental traffic jams. On June 30, 1984, 25 years later to the day, summer service was restored by the Cape Cod & Hyannis Railroad, which had been running excursion trains between Hyannis, Buzzards Bay, and Falmouth for several summers. The ex-New Haven track is owned by the commonwealth of Massachusetts. South of Middleboro CC&H shares the track with Amtrak's summer-only New York-Cape Cod trains and Bay Colony freight trains; north of Middleboro Conrail provides freight service. At Buzzards Bay trains cross the Cape Cod Canal on the world's longest vertical-lift bridge.

Trains operate from the Braintree terminal of the Red Line of Boston's subway system; the Hyannis station and the company's offices are at 252 Main Street in the center of town. Staff are on premises year-round. Trains also stop at Holbrook, Brockton, Bridgewater, Middleboro, Wareham, Buzzards Bay, Sandwich, and West Barnstable. Running time between Braintree and Hyannis is 2 hours 25 minutes (a bit less for some trains).

In addition to the Braintree-Hyannis trains, the CC&H operates excursion trains between Hyannis, Sandwich, and Buzzards Bay and offers numerous package tours and charter trips. Trains carry coaches, first-class parlor cars, and cafe and lounge cars offering meals, snacks, and beverages. Food and lodging can be found at Hyannis and at other points along the line.

Locomotives	3 diesel
Cars	Ex-Lackawanna coaches
Displays	Pennsylvania coach used as museum, box car, cabooses, Fairmont speeder
Schedule	Weekends Memorial Day through October, leave Lee 10:30 a.m. and 2:00 p.m.; Fridays in July and August, leave Lee 6:00 p.m. Charter trips operated.
Fares	Adults $7, children 5-12 $4, age 60 and over, $6. Checks and credit cards accepted. Group discounts available.
Memberships	Write for information.
Special events	Berkshire County Day, Columbia County Day, Americana Day (July 4), Halloween Special, Friday evening Cabaret Specials in July and August
Nearby attractions	Norman Rockwell Museum, Hancock Shaker Village, Tanglewood (home of the Berkshire Music Festival), Jacob's Pillow Dance Festival, Berkshire Theater Festival
Address	P. O. Box 298, Lee, MA 01238
Phone	(413) 243-2872

P & ⊼ 🎁

BERKSHIRE SCENIC RAILWAY MUSEUM

The Berkshire Scenic Railway Museum, established in 1984, operates excursion trains over 15 miles of the former Berkshire line of the New Haven Railroad along the Housatonic River between Lee and Great Barrington, Massachusetts. The route's last regular passenger trains, which ran weekends only between New York and Pittsfield, Massachusetts, were discontinued when Amtrak took over the nation's passenger trains in 1971.

The round trip from Lee takes 2 hours 40 minutes, and passengers may also board and detrain at Stockbridge and Housatonic, continuing on the next train. Tickets can be purchased at the museum and gift shop in Lee (at 41 Canal Street) or on the train. Soft drinks are available on the train, and box suppers for the Friday evening trips can be purchased until 30 minutes before departure. Restaurants and snack bars are adjacent to the station in Lee, and food and lodging can be found throughout the Berkshire area — reservations for lodging are advisable.

Cars	2 open streetcars
Dates open	Park is open year-round.
Schedule	Daily, Memorial Day-Columbus Day
Admission	Free
Fares	Free
Nearby attractions	Lexington, Concord, Boston
Address	169 Merrimac Street, Lowell, MA 01852
Phone	(617) 459-1000

P 🎁

LOWELL NATIONAL HISTORICAL PARK

Abundant water power and the new technology of the power loom combined in the early 1800s to create America's first industrial city, Lowell, Massachusetts. The textile industry moved to the South after World War Two, and decline overtook Lowell (and many other New England cities). In the 1970s high-tech industry began moving into the area, Lowell began to boom again, and the area of the textile mills and power canals became first a Heritage State Park and then a National Historical Park.

A mile of a Boston & Maine industrial track was electrified and extended, and two open streetcars were constructed to operate along the track and tie together the areas of the park. If you are driving, follow U. S. 3 or Interstate 495 to the Lowell Connector; leave the Connector at Exit 5N, Thorndike Street, and follow signs to the parking area for the historical park. You can also take a Massachusetts Bay Transportation Authority train from North Station, Boston — hourly on weekdays; every two hours on weekends and holidays. The 26-mile ride takes about 40 minutes. There are numerous restaurants in and around the park area; lodging is available in and around Lowell. The park facilities are partially accessible to the handicapped.

Displays	More than 2000 model trains
Dates open	Daily 10 a.m.-5 p.m., except Thanksgiving, Christmas, and New Year's Day
Admission	Adults $3, children 5-12 $1.50, age 65 and over $2.50. Credit cards accepted. Group discounts available (reservations needed for groups).
Memberships	Write for information.
Special events	Hobby Days (January 24 and 25), Antique Train Days (February 14 and 15), Children's Day (March 22), Mother's Day (May 10), Father's Day (June 14), Amtrak Days (July 11 and 12), Tom Thumb Days (August 15 and 16), Old Folks' Day (September 6), Christmas Festival (November 7-January 3, 1988), plus swap meets April 26 and October 25 at Meredith Williams Middle School, South Street, Bridgewater
Nearby attractions	Cape Cod, Plymouth, Edaville Railroad, Cape Cod & Hyannis Railroad
Address	49 Plymouth Street, Middleboro, MA 02346-1197
Phone	(617) 947-5303

A&D TOY-TRAIN VILLAGE AND RAILWAY MUSEUM

More than 2000 toy trains of all kinds from around the world are on display at the A&D Toy-Train Village and Railway Museum. The museum began with a Christmas train set that soon outgrew an apartment, then a basement, then a barn, and is now housed in a former supermarket. Middleboro is in southeastern Massachusetts between Taunton and Plymouth and between Brockton and Fall River. To reach the museum, go north on Routes 18 and 28 2 miles from the Middleboro traffic circle, junction of 18 and 28 with U. S. 44. Turn left (west) on Plymouth Street; the museum is at 49 Plymouth Street.

EDAVILLE RAILROAD

When Maine's 2-foot-gauge Bridgton & Harrison ceased operation in 1941, its rolling stock was purchased by Ellis D. Atwood, who had a large cranberry plantation at South Carver, Massachusetts. Atwood moved the equipment to Massachusetts at the end of World War Two, laid a 5½-mile loop of track on the dikes around his cranberry bogs, and set the railroad to work hauling cranberries and sand and, more often, people. Word spread, and soon Atwood was in the tourist-railroad business. Atwood died in 1950, but the Edaville Railroad (the name came from his initials) thrived and grew, adding a museum and various tourist attractions and becoming separate from the cranberry business.

In addition to the 30-minute, 5½-mile train ride, Edaville offers children's rides, a petting zoo, and entertainment. The Edaville Railroad is southeast of Middleboro and southwest of Plymouth on Massachusetts Route 58 south of U. S. 44 and north of I-495/State Route 25. Edaville has a restaurant and a snack bar; food and lodging are available in Plymouth, about 15 miles northeast.

Locomotives	4 steam, 2 diesel
Cars	Wooden coaches, open cars, cabooses
Displays	Boston & Maine 2-6-0 and *Flying Yankee*
Dates open	Weekends in May, noon-5 p.m.; Daily June-Labor Day 10-5:30; Labor Day through October weekends 10:30-5 with steam, Monday-Friday 10:30-3 with diesel power; November through first Sunday after New Year's Day, except Thanksgiving and Christmas, weekends 2-9, weekdays 4-9
Admission	Adults $7.50, children 3-12 $5, senior citizens $6. Admission includes train ride. Checks accepted. Group discounts available (reservations necessary for groups).
Memberships	Write for information.
Special events	Civil War Weekend (first weekend in June), Railfans Weekend (third weekend in June), Family Fun Week (end of June through beginning of July), Antique and Classic Auto Show (third Sunday in August), Christmas Festival (November-New Year's)
Nearby attractions	Plymouth, Cape Cod, A&D Toy-Train Village, Cape Cod & Hyannis Railroad
Address	P. O. Box 7, South Carver, MA 02366
Phone	(617) 866-4526

South Carver

Locomotives	Diesel hood units
Cars	Streamlined coaches, cafe car, round-end observation car
Schedule	May-October, several Sundays a month, plus one December trip. Charter trains available.
Fares	Depends on itinerary. Fares on the Zoo Train to Providence, for example, are adults $14.95, children through age 12 $9.95, observation car $17.95. Babies not occupying a seat ride free; persons 60 and over receive a 10 percent discount. Discounts are available for groups of 25 or more. Tickets must be purchased in advance by mail; checks accepted.
Nearby attractions	Old Sturbridge Village
Address	P. O. Box 1188, Worcester, MA 01601
Phone	(617) 799-4474; 755-4000 for recorded information

Tom Nelligan

PROVIDENCE & WORCESTER RAILROAD

The Providence & Worcester was opened between the cities of its name in 1847, and by the turn of the century it was part of the New Haven. In 1970 the P&W requested independence from New Haven successor Penn Central and in 1973 got it. It has purchased several former New Haven and Boston & Maine lines in Rhode Island, Connecticut, and Massachusetts, and has acquired freight rights on Amtrak between Providence & Old Saybrook.

In 1983 the P&W began operating weekend excursion trains using former Union Pacific coaches and dining car and an ex-Northern Pacific observation car. The railroad's 1986 schedule showed excursion trains operating up to three Sundays a month to such diverse destinations as Roger Williams Park Zoo in Providence, Rhode Island;

the Valley Railroad; Mystic Seaport; the U. S. Naval Submarine Base in Groton, Conn.; plus fall foliage and Santa Claus trains. Depending on the destination, trips take 2 to 10 hours. The trains are air-conditioned and heated and carry a dining car with snack service and an observation car offering first-class service. In addition there is a souvenir shop in one of the coaches. All trains depart from the P&W yard at 382 Southbridge Street in Worcester, Mass., half a mile from Exit 11 of I-290. Departure time depends on the destination; most are between 8 and 11:30 a.m. Handicapped persons may have some difficulty boarding and detraining; advance inquiry is advisable. Food and lodging are available in Worcester.

THE QUARTER-SIZE LINE

Locomotives	4 diesel
Cars	Freight cars
Schedule	May 22-September 7, 1987, Monday-Saturday 11 a.m.-7 p.m., Sunday 1-6; then weekends through October, 1-5 p.m.
Fares	Adults $2, children 18 months to 12 years $1.50, age 65 and over $1.80. Group discounts available.
Special events	Halloween Spook Train Ride; many days have a special theme such as free ride for fathers, half fare for grandparents.
Nearby attractions	Village of Frankenmuth
Address	7065 Dixie Highway, Bridgeport, MI 48722
Phone	(517) 777-3480

JUNCTION VALLEY RAILROAD

The Junction Valley Railroad has 1¼ miles of 14⅛"-gauge track. Trains loop around a lake and then pass through woods to a picnic area with concession stands and playground equipment. The ride takes about 20 minutes. Children must be accompanied by adults. Guided tours are available of the railroad's shop, where all the equipment was built, and staff is on premises year-round. The railroad is located a few miles southeast of Saginaw, Michigan. From Flint and south, leave I-75 at Exit 136, go east to the first traffic signal, then north 6 miles on Dixie Highway. From Saginaw and north, use Exit 144 from I-75 and follow Dixie Highway southeast 2 miles to just beyond Junction Road. Restaurants and lodging can be found in Bridgeport and Frankenmuth, 5 miles east.

Bridgeport

Locomotives	3 steam
Cars	Open cars; occasionally 2 historic cars
Dates open	Daily 9-5; closed Thanksgiving, Christmas, and New Year's Day
Schedule	Train operates April 1-October 31
Admission	Adults $8 to museum, $8 to village; children 5-12 $4/$4; senior citizens $7/$7. Credit cards accepted. Group discounts available.
Fares	Adults $1.50, children 5-12 $1
Memberships	Write for information.
Special events	The museum and village have numerous special events but none that are railroad-oriented.
Nearby attractions	Detroit
Address	P. O. Box 1970, Dearborn, MI 48121
Phone	(313) 271-1620; 271-1976 for recorded information; (800) 338-0125 (9-5 weekdays from the Midwest, New York, and Pennsylvania)

Ernest L. Novak

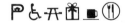

HENRY FORD MUSEUM AND GREENFIELD VILLAGE

The Henry Ford Museum displays the changes in American technology from 1800 to 1950, from an agricultural society to an industrial one. Adjacent to the museum is Greenfield Village, a re-creation of a village of the late 1800s consisting of historic buildings moved there from much of the U. S. The project was begun by Henry Ford as a tribute to his friend Thomas Edison and was dedicated in 1929. It and the museum are now the property of the Edison Institute and are not connected with the Ford Motor Company.

Steam-powered trains circle Greenfield Village on a 2-mile loop of track. The ride takes about 20 minutes. The museum contains several small older locomotives, some original, some replicas, a Chesapeake & Ohio 2-6-6-6, several older passenger cars, and a collection of railroad hardware, notably lanterns, rail, and couplers.

Dearborn is located about halfway between downtown Detroit and the Detroit airport. The museum is on Oakwood Boulevard no more than 2 miles from the Southfield Freeway (Route 39) and Exit 206 of the Detroit Industrial Freeway (I-94). The museum is accessible to the handicapped; not all the buildings in Greenfield Village are. The museum and the village have several restaurants and snack bars; food and lodging can be found in Dearborn.

DETROIT DEPARTMENT OF TRANSPORTATION

Detroit's last streetcar line shut down in 1956, but twenty years later streetcars returned to operate along nine blocks of Washington Boulevard in downtown Detroit. Instead of the streamlined PCC cars that were sold to Mexico came six antique 4-wheel cars from Lisbon, Portugal, five closed cars and one open. They were later joined by two others, one of them a British double-deck car. It and the open car operate only during the summer. The line was extended to the Renaissance Center in 1980. The total length of the meter-gauge track is 1½ miles; the ride from the Renaissance Center to Grand Circus Park takes 12 minutes. Food and lodging are available: The trolley runs past three of Detroit's most elegant hotels.

Cars	8 streetcars
Schedule	Year-round, every 12 minutes, 7 a.m.-6 p.m. Monday-Friday, 10-6 on weekends; on special occasions such as summer ethnic festivals cars operate to 11 p.m.
Fares	45 cents; infants and senior citizens free
Nearby attractions	Greektown, Trapper's Alley, Renaissance Center, Henry Ford Museum and Greenfield Village
Address	1301 East Warren, Detroit, MI 48207
Phone	(313) 833-7365; 933-1300 for schedule information

Locomotives	2 steam, 2 diesel
Cars	Coaches, open cars
Dates open	May 20 to September 7, Monday-Friday 10 a.m.-5:30 p.m.; weekends and holidays from 11 to 6:30; also Fridays, Saturdays, and Sundays in December from 3 to 9 p.m.
Schedule	Hourly departures, Monday-Friday 11-4, weekends and holidays noon-5
Admission	Adults $5.95, children 4-12 $3.95 (under 4 free), age 60 and over $4.95. Parking $1. Checks accepted. Group

	discounts available (reservations are advisable). Lower prices during Christmas season.
Memberships	Write for information.
Special events	Railfans Weekend, Christmas at Crossroads, Capt. Phogg Balloon Festival, Michigan Storytellers Festival
Nearby attractions	Flint Cultural Center, Pennywhistle Place, Frankenmuth
Address	G-5055 Branch Road, Flint, MI 48506
Phone	(313) 736-7100; 736-3220 for recorded information

HUCKLEBERRY RAILROAD

A few miles north of Flint, Michigan, the Genesee County Parks and Recreation Commission operates Crossroads Village, a replica of an 1800s-era country town, complete with the 3-foot-gauge Huckleberry Railroad. The train makes a 45-minute, 10-mile trip through the Genesee Recreation Area. Usual motive power is an ex-Alaska Railroad 4-6-0; two diesels stand in reserve, and Rio Grande 2-8-2

No. 464 is likely to be operable in 1987. Staff is on the premises year-round. The grounds are fully accessible to the handicapped. Crossroads Village has a cafe and a snack bar. Restaurants can be found in Genesee and Flint; lodging in Flint. To reach Crossroads Village, use Exit 11, Carpenter Road, from I-475 in the northern part of Flint. Drive east approximately a mile, then turn north on Bray Road.

Locomotives	1 diesel
Cars	2 Chicago L cars, 1 North Shore interurban, 1 Detroit PCC car
Dates open	Mt. Clemens Depot Museum: Sundays, 2-4 p.m.
Schedule	Mid-May through September, Sundays, leave Caboose Depot at 1, 2, 3, and 4 p.m. Charter trips operated.
Admission	Mt. Clemens Depot Museum: free
Fares	Adults $3, children 6-12 $1.75 (under 6 free). Admission to the Selfridge Military Air Museum is an additional 50 cents for adults, 25 cents for children. Group discounts available; reservations are required for groups. Checks accepted.
Memberships	Write for information.
Special events	Farm-City Week, Air Show
Nearby attractions	Detroit, Henry Ford Museum and Greenfield Village
Address	P. O. Box 12, Fraser, MI 48026
Phone	(313) 466-5035; 463-1863 for recorded information

MICHIGAN TRANSIT MUSEUM

The Michigan Transit Museum operates 4½ miles of track extending east from Mt. Clemens, Michigan, to Selfridge Air National Guard Base. The museum's usual train consists of an Alco S1 diesel switcher and two Chicago elevated cars. Eastbound the locomotive functions solely as a generator providing current for the motors in the two L cars; on the return trip the locomotive pulls the cars. Trains depart from the Caboose Depot on the east side of Gratiot Avenue (Michigan Route 3) north of downtown Mt. Clemens between Joy Boulevard and Hall Road (Route 59) — between Exits 237 and 240 of I-94. The headquarters of the Michigan Transit Museum are in the former Grand Trunk station, scene of Thomas Edison's short career in railroading. The building is at Cass and Grand Avenues west of downtown Mt. Clemens. The museum is accessible to the handicapped; the train ride is not. Food and lodging can be found in Mt. Clemens, about 20 miles northeast of Detroit.

Locomotives	1 gasoline, 1 diesel
Cars	Open cars; closed cars in September and October
Schedule	June 15-30, daily; July and August, Friday, Saturday and Sunday; and September 1-October 6, daily: leaves 10:30 a.m., returns at 5 p.m.; July and August, Monday-Thursday leaves 10 and 11:30, returns at 4:30 and 6:30. Charter trips available.
Fares	Train and boat, adults $10, children 5-12 $4.50. Checks accepted. Group discounts available.
Nearby attractions	Hiawatha National Forest, Pictured Rocks National Lakeshore
Address	115 East Avenue A, Newberry, MI 49868
Phone	(906) 876-2311

TOONERVILLE TROLLEY

The Toonerville Trolley is a 24-inch-gauge railroad that carries tourists 5½ miles from the highway to a boat dock, where connection is made with a sightseeing boat on the Tahquamenom River. The rail portion of the trip begins at Soo Junction, off Michigan Route 28 between Newberry and Hulbert in the eastern part of Michigan's Upper Peninsula. The destination of the boat trip is Upper Tahquamenom Falls. One trip a day is operated from mid-June to the beginning of October, except Monday through Thursday in July and August, when two trips run. Warm clothing is advised for trips toward the end of the season. Snacks are available at Soo Junction and on the boat. Restaurants and lodging can be found in Newberry; the cities of Sault Ste. Marie, Mich., and Ontario, are 57 miles east. Access is possible for the handicapped; however, walking is required at the end of the boat trip.

Locomotives	2 diesel
Cars	3 coaches, 2 open cars, caboose
Schedule	Memorial Day-late fall
Fares	Adults $5, children under 13 $4, age 65 and over $4. Checks and credit cards accepted. Group discounts available.
Nearby attractions	Sleeping Bear Dunes National Lakeshore, Manistee National Forest, 15"-gauge steam train at Clinch Park Zoo in Traverse City
Address	9945 Carter Road, Traverse City, MI 49684
Phone	(616) 946-3937; 947-6667 for recorded information

LEELANAU SCENIC RAILROAD

The Leelanau Scenic Railroad operates excursion trains from Traverse City north through Leelanau County to Suttons Bay, Omena, and Northport, Michigan, 31 miles from Traverse City. The line was once part of the Manistee & Northeastern Railway, then belonged to the Chesapeake & Ohio. Snacks are available on the train. Restaurants and lodging can be found in Traverse City, Suttons Bay, Omena, and Northport. Traverse City is about two-thirds of the way up the west side of Michigan's Lower Peninsula.

Locomotives	1 steam, 1 diesel
Cars	2 streetcars, converted box cars
Dates open	Wednesday-Sunday, 10 a.m.-7 p.m.; streetcars leave the reception center approximately every hour.
Schedule	Trains operate May 23-Labor Day
Admission	Summer, adults $5.25, children 6-17 $3, age 65 and over $4.75. Winter, adults $3, children $1. Checks and credit cards accepted. Group discounts available.
Memberships	Write for information.
Special events	Ethnic weekends, International Polka Festival
Nearby attractions	Forest History Center, Hill Annex Mine Tour, Minnesota Museum of Mining, Paulucci Space Theater, Soudan Mine State Park
Address	P. O. Box 392, Chisholm, MN 55719
Phone	(218) 254-3321

IRONWORLD USA

Ironworld USA is a theme park in Minnesota's Iron Range. It is sponsored by Minnesota's Department of Iron Range Resources and is an outgrowth of the Iron Range Interpretive Center that was established in 1977. Plans call for a large hotel and a re-created Iron Range town of the 1920s. A train carries visitors from the reception center around the rim of an open-pit mine to the town area. The ride is in two parts. Two streetcars from Melbourne, Australia, negotiate a 6 percent grade between the reception center and a transfer station, where on Fridays and weekends passengers transfer to a steam train (streetcars run the entire distance at other times). The streetcars were refurbished and the passenger cars were converted from box cars by the staff of the Lake Superior Museum of Transportation in Duluth; the steam locomotive is on loan from the Duluth museum. Ironworld is 5 miles east of Hibbing on U. S. 169. It is about 1½ hours from Duluth and 3½ hours from the Twin Cities.

Locomotives	2 diesel
Cars	Coaches, gondola
Displays	GN *William Crooks*, NP *Minnetonka*, DM&IR 227, CMStP&P 10200, rotary snow plow, passenger and freight cars
Dates open	Year-round, daily 10 a.m.-5 p.m., except winter Sundays opens at 1
Schedule	Some summer weekends, leave Duluth Zoo noon, 2, and 4. Charter trips operated.
Admission	Museum, including trolley ride: adults $3, children 6-17 $1.50, age 60 and over $2.50. Group discounts available. Checks accepted.
Fares	Excursion train: adults $3.50, children to age 12 $1.50, age 60 and over $3
Memberships	Write for information.
Special events	Excursion trains
Nearby attractions	Canal Park Marine Museum, Duluth-Superior harbor cruise, Glensheen House Tour

Address	506 West Michigan Street, Duluth, MN 55802
Phone	(218) 727-0687; 722-3008 for recorded information

LAKE SUPERIOR MUSEUM OF TRANSPORTATION

Duluth Union Depot saw its last pre-Amtrak train in May 1969. The building, a fine example of French Norman architecture, was designated a National Historic Site in 1971 and was purchased from the Burlington Northern that same year. It soon became the property of St. Louis County, and work began to renovate the building and transform it into a cultural center. The building now serves as an art museum and a theater — and houses an excellent railroad museum.

A train shed covers the station's track area, protecting the locomotives and cars on display and allowing year-round viewing of the displays. Locomotives displayed include Great Northern 4-4-0 *William Crooks*; Northern Pacific's first engine, *Minnetonka*; Duluth, Missabe & Iron Range 2-8-8-4 No. 227; and Milwaukee Road boxcab electric 10200. The collection is filled out by numerous passenger and freight cars and pieces of maintenance of way equipment. Two 4-wheel streetcars from Lisbon, Portugal, operate on ¼ mile of track on the museum grounds.

The museum is in downtown Duluth, easily accessible from I-35. Food and lodging are available within one block. The museum is accessible to the handicapped, and tours for the sight- or hearing-impaired are available if requested in advance.

The Lake Superior & Mississippi Railroad, an affiliate of the museum, operates excursion trains on certain summer weekends. They operate from the Duluth Zoo on a 1½-hour trip over 5½ miles of track along the St. Louis River. To reach the zoo, take Exit 251A, Cody Street, from I-35 northbound; Exit 251B, Grand Avenue, from I-35 southbound.

Locomotives	1 steam
Cars	Coaches, combine; 2 streetcars
Schedule	Memorial Day-Labor Day: Monday-Friday 6:30 p.m.-dusk; Saturday 3:30-dusk; Sunday and holidays 12:30-dusk. Charter trips operated.
Fares	Streetcar: 50 cents per person (age 2 and under free). Checks accepted. Group discounts available for charter trips. Write for information on steam trips.
Memberships	Individuals $20, families $25, includes bimonthly magazine and eligibility to operate streetcar; associate $15, magazine only
Nearby attractions	Tyrone Guthrie Theater, Hennepin County Historical Society and Museum, State Capitol (in St. Paul)
Address	P. O. Box 1300, Hopkins, MN 55343
Phone	(612) 729-2428

P &. ⊼

MINNESOTA TRANSPORTATION MUSEUM

The primary operating exhibit of the Minnesota Transportation Museum is the 1-mile Como-Harriet streetcar line at West 42nd Street and Queen Avenue South in Minneapolis. Two cars, Twin City Rapid Transit 1300 and Duluth Street Railway 265, operate over a restored portion of track between Lake Harriet and Lake Calhoun. To reach the site from downtown, follow Hennepin Avenue and Route 20. From the south use the Xerxes Avenue South (Route 31) exit from Route 62.

The Minnesota Transportation Museum also operates steam-powered excursion trains using Northern Pacific 4-6-0 No. 328 (pictured on the cover of this book) over railroads in the Minneapolis-St. Paul area and on a 6-mile line west of Stillwater.

Locomotives	2 diesel
Cars	Dining cars, dome lounge cars
Schedule	Open at 6:30 p.m., departure at 7:30 Tuesday-Saturday; noon trips on Saturday and Sunday. Reservations required.
Fares	$39.50. Checks and credit cards accepted. Group discounts available.
Nearby attractions	Canterbury Downs Minnesota Railway Museum, Chanhassen Dinner Theater
Address	4100 Sunset Drive, Spring Park, MN 55384-0354
Phone	(612) 471-0977

Steve Glischinski

MINNETONKA ZEPHYR LIMITED

Minnetonka Zephyr Limited operates a dinner train out of Spring Park, Minnesota, about 20 miles west of Minneapolis on Route 15 southwest of Wayzata. The train carries dome lounge cars, for before-dinner cocktails and hors d'oeuvres, and dining cars, where dinner is served. During dinner the train travels along the shore of Lake Minnetonka and west to Mayer, about 12 miles, then returns to Spring Park. The trip takes 3¼ hours. The tracks belong to Dakota Rail and were once Great Northern's branch to Hutchinson, Minn.

Locomotive	1 steam
Cars	Ex-Illinois Central and ex-Lackawanna coaches
Schedule	Operates approximately one weekend per month April-October with departures at 1 and 3 p.m. — more trips for a few special events. Charter trips available.
Fares	Adults $5, children under 13 $4, age 62 and over $4.50. Group discounts available. Checks accepted.
Memberships	Write for information.
Special events	Amory Railroad Festival, Redlands Festival, Rod Brasfield Festival, Railfan Weekend, Fall Color Specials, Halloween Ghost Train
Nearby attractions	Tennessee-Tombigbee Waterway, antebellum homes, Elvis Presley's birthplace
Address	Highway 25 South, Amory, MS 38821
Phone	(601) 256-5298

P & ⌂

MAGNOLIA STATE RAILWAY

The Mississippian Railway, a line from Amory to Fulton, Mississippi, operated with steam power until 1968, when its last steam locomotive, No. 77, a 2-8-0, was sold to the North Alabama Railroad Club. The locomotive was built for the Jonesboro, Lake City & Eastern and joined the Frisco roster when that road acquired the JLC&E in 1925. It was purchased by the Mississippian Railway in 1947, and it has returned there to power excursion trains. Trains operate from Smithville, 8 miles northeast of Amory, to Mt. Peak, highest point on the line, and then return, for a total of 15½ miles. Amory is on the eastern border of Mississippi north of Columbus, about halfway between Memphis, Tennessee, and Birmingham, Alabama. Food and lodging can be found in Amory and Fulton; there are also restaurants in Smithville.

Amory

Locomotives	2 steam, 3 gasoline
Cars	Flat cars with benches, 1 steel passenger car, freight cars
Schedule	Sundays May-October, except when it's raining; departures at 1, 1:40, 2:20, 3, 3:40, and 4:20 p.m. Charter trips available.
Fares	$1.50 (children under 3 free). Checks accepted. Group rate, $1.25 per person.
Memberships	$15 per year; students $7.50
Special events	Members' Day (second Sunday of October)
Nearby attractions	National Museum of Transport, Six Flags Over Mid-America
Address	1569 Ville Angela Lane, Hazelwood, MO 63042
Phone	(314) 587-3538 (Sundays after 11 a.m. only)

WABASH, FRISCO & PACIFIC MINI-STEAM TOURIST RAILWAY

The Wabash, Frisco & Pacific is a 12″-gauge steam-powered railroad that operates as authentically as possible. The railroad was begun in 1939 at a site near the St. Louis airport. Rising land values forced relocation in 1959, and in 1961 a new railroad was built along the Missouri Pacific's original roadbed. Trains operate over 1.3 miles of track through woodlands along the Meramec River. Unique to the Wabash, Frisco & Pacific is the crossing of Grand Avenue, protected by full-size flashers.

Glencoe is 25 miles west-southwest of downtown St. Louis on Route 109 north of I-44/U. S. 50. From Route 109 take Old State Road east to the Glencoe post office. Turn right to Washington Avenue; follow Washington and Grand approximately half a mile to the Wabash, Frisco & Pacific station. Food and lodging are available in Eureka 3½ miles away. There is a soda vending machine at the station. Access to the trains may be difficult for the handicapped, but train crews offer assistance as needed.

Locomotives	1 steam
Cars	Ex-Illinois Central coaches, ex-Missouri Pacific caboose
Schedule	April-October, Saturdays and holidays leave Jackson for Gordonville at 8:30 a.m. and 3:00 p.m., for Delta at 10 a.m.; Sundays to Gordonville at 1 and 2:30, to Delta at 4:30
Fares	Jackson-Gordonville round trip $5; Jackson-Delta round trip $10. Children under 5 free. Group discount available. Checks and credit cards accepted.
Nearby attractions	Oldtimers Agricultural Museum & Park
Address	P. O. Box 244, Jackson, MO 63755
Phone	(314) 243-1688

℗ ♿ 🛉 🎁 ☕

ST. LOUIS, IRON MOUNTAIN & SOUTHERN RAILWAY

The name of a long-ago predecessor of the Missouri Pacific was revived for a tourist railroad operating over the rails of the Jackson & Southern Railroad, a short line established to operate a former MP branch from Delta to Jackson, Missouri. The St. Louis, Iron Mountain & Southern operates trains from Jackson to Gordonville, 5 miles, and to Delta, 18 miles; round trips take 75 minutes and 3½ hours respectively. Trains depart from the intersection of Highways 25, 72, and U. S. 61 in Jackson. Jackson is about 110 miles southsoutheast of St. Louis on I-55 and about 6 miles northwest of Cape Girardeau. Restaurants and motels can be found in Jackson and Cape Girardeau.

Jackson

Displays	One of the largest collections of locomotives and cars in the U. S.
Dates open	Daily 9 a.m.-5 p.m.; closed Thanksgiving, Christmas, and New Year's Day
Admission	Adults $2, children 5-12 $1 (under 5 free), age 65 and over $1. Credit cards and local checks accepted. Group discounts available; reservations required for groups.
Memberships	Transport Museum Association — write for information.
Nearby attractions	Wabash, Frisco & Pacific Railway, Six Flags Over Mid-America
Address	3015 Barrett Station Road, St. Louis, MO 63122
Phone	(314) 965-7998

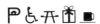

NATIONAL MUSEUM OF TRANSPORT

The rescue and preservation of a mule-drawn streetcar in 1944 was the beginning of the National Museum of Transport. The museum soon acquired other exhibits and became one of the largest and most diverse in the U. S. In 1979 operation of the museum was taken over by the St. Louis County Department of Parks & Recreation.

The locomotive collection ranges from industrial-size switchers and a Reading inspection locomotive with a 2-2-2 wheel arrangement to a Union Pacific Big Boy and a Norfolk & Western 2-8-8-2. The electric locomotives represent both interurbans and standard "steam" railroads, and among the diesels are Baltimore & Ohio 50, the first non-articulated mainline diesel passenger locomotive; Burlington 9908, *Silver Charger*, the last of the "shovel-nose" *Zephyr*

units; and one unit of Electro-Motive 103, the Model FT demonstrator that was the first large mainline freight diesel. The passenger car, freight car, and trolley collections are similarly extensive; in addition the museum has collections of automobiles, buses, and trucks.

The museum is located on a section of the original right of way of the Missouri Pacific northwest of the intersection of I-270 and I-44. Using I-270 from the north, take the Big Bend Road exit, go west to Barrett Station Road, then north to the museum. From the south, take the Dougherty Ferry Road exit, go west to Barrett Station Road, then south to the museum. (Neither exit from I-270 has ramps in all directions.) Food and lodging are available throughout the area.

Locomotives	4 diesel
Cars	Coaches, flat cars with benches, cabooses
Schedule	April-October, second Sunday of the month, departures at 1, 2, 3, and 4 p.m.
Fares	Free, except for hayride; donations accepted
Memberships	$15 per year
Special events	Moonlight Train Ride, Hayride On The Train (second Sunday in November)
Nearby attractions	Gateway Arch, Missouri Botanical Garden
Address	3422 Osage Street, St. Louis, MO 63118
Phone	(314) 752-3148

ST. LOUIS & CHAIN OF ROCKS RAILROAD

The St. Louis Water Works Railway was opened between the Baden section of St. Louis and a water works at Chain of Rocks in 1902. The railroad soon developed into a steam-powered freight railroad and a streetcar line with a scenic route serving a large city park. Passenger service was discontinued in 1955. A group of railroad enthusiasts looking for a site for an operating museum approached the St. Louis Water Department, which was amenable — even enthusiastic — about the project. Excursion trains began running in 1972, and the St. Louis & Chain of Rocks Railroad was organized in 1976.

Trains operate on 3 miles of track along Riverview Boulevard between Burlington Northern Junction and Mississippi River Dam No. 27, largest rock-fill dam in the U. S. At the south end of the run there is a distant view of the St. Louis skyline and the Gateway Arch. The boarding area is at Briscoe Station on Riverview Boulevard at Lookaway Drive, 1½ miles south of the I-270 bridge over the Mississippi River. Take the Columbia Bottom Road-Riverview Drive exit from I-270 at the west end of the Mississippi River bridge, and drive south along Riverview to the station. Food and lodging are available throughout the area; lemonade is available at the station.

Locomotives	Speeders
Cars	Open cars
Displays	Turn-of-the-century cars and locomotives
Dates open	Memorial Day-Labor Day
Schedule	Trains operate mid-June to Labor Day, hourly 10 a.m.-6 p.m., weather permitting. Charter trips available.
Admission	Age 12 and over $3 (under 12 free), age 65 and over $2.50. Includes train ride. Credit cards accepted. Group discounts available.
Nearby attractions	Virginia City, Nevada City, Yellowstone National Park
Address	P. O. Box 338, Virginia City, MT 59755
Phone	(406) 843-5377

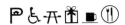

BOVEY RESTORATIONS

One of the attractions of Nevada City, Montana, a restored gold-mining town near Virginia City, is the Alder Gulch Short Line, which carries passengers over 1½ miles of track between Nevada City and Virginia City. At Nevada City is a railroad museum which includes 4 locomotives and 25 freight and passenger cars, among them 5 Soo Line passenger cars of the early 1900s, the chapel car *Saint Paul*, and possibly the largest collection of cars built by Barney & Smith. Staff is on the premises year-round. Food and lodging are available in Virginia City and in the Nevada City restoration. Virginia City is on State Route 287 southwest of Bozeman and southeast of Butte and about 70 highway miles from each.

Locomotives	1 steam
Cars	Coach, freight cars
Dates open	May-September, daily 9 a.m.-6 p.m.; October-April, Monday-Saturday 9-5, Sunday 1-5
Schedule	Train operates May-September; Monday-Saturday at 11, noon, 1:30, and 3:30, also 4:30 if needed; Sunday continuously from 11
Admission	May-September, adults $4, children 7-16 $2 (under 7 free). October-April, adults $2, children 7-6 $1. Checks accepted.
Fares	Adults $1.50, children 7-16 75 cents
Memberships	Individual, $10 per year; family, $15.
Special events	Memorial Day and July 4th celebrations
Nearby attractions	Harold Warp Pioneer Village
Address	3133 West Highway 34, Grand Island, NE 68801
Phone	(308) 384-1380

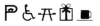

STUHR MUSEUM OF THE PRAIRIE PIONEER

The Stuhr Museum, operated by Hall County, interprets prairie life of the latter half of the nineteenth century with a log cabin farm and a re-creation of a small prairie town. Part of the town exhibit is the 3-foot-gauge Nebraska Midland Railroad, which offers a 3½-mile ride around the museum grounds. The train is pulled by former White Pass & Yukon No. 69, a 2-8-0 built in 1908. The museum also has exhibits of Indian culture and antique automobiles and farm machinery, plus a herd of buffaloes and 10 acres of corn. The museum is on U. S. Routes 34 and 281 between I-80 and the city of Grand Island. Restaurants and motels can be found in Grand Island, 3 miles north.

Locomotives	2 steam	Fares	Train: Adults $1.50, children 2-12 $1 (under 2 free)	Address	Deer Park Boulevard and 10th Street, Omaha, NE 68107
Cars	Open coaches, caboose				
Dates open	Daily, April-October	Memberships	Zoo — write for information.	Phone	(402) 733-8401; 733-8400 for recorded information
Schedule	Train operates weekends only in April, May, September, and October; daily June-August	Special events	Membership Day — zoo members may ride train free all day.		
		Nearby attractions	Union Pacific Historical Museum, General Dodge House, Western Heritage Museum, Sarpy County Historical Museum, Children's Museum		
Admission	Zoo: Adults $4.50, children $2.50 (under 6 free), senior citizens $3. Group discounts available.				

OMAHA ZOO RAILROAD

Circling the grounds of the Henry Doorly Zoo in Omaha is 3 miles of 30″-gauge track, home rails for a pair of steam locomotives, one a 5/8-scale replica of Union Pacific 119 (one of the participants in the 1869 Golden Spike ceremony) and the other an 0-6-2T built in 1890 and first used in Austria and later in Romania. The railroad is oper-

ated by the Omaha Zoological Society; it is maintained with the help of the Union Pacific, which is headquartered in Omaha. The zoo is one block southeast of the 13th Street (U. S. 73-75) exit of I-80 near the Missouri River.

Dates open	Monday-Friday, 9 a.m.-5 p.m.; Saturday 9-1. Closed Sundays and holidays.
Admission	Free
Nearby attractions	Omaha Zoo Railroad, General Dodge House, Western Heritage Museum, Sarpy County Historical Museum, Children's Museum
Address	1416 Dodge Street, Omaha, NE 68179
Phone	(402) 271-3530

UNION PACIFIC HISTORICAL MUSEUM

The Union Pacific Railroad claims a closer connection to the history of the United States than any other railroad. UP was one of the two companies that built the first railroad to the Pacific; completed in 1869, that railroad was the sole thread that connected East and West for more than a decade. UP founded its museum in 1921 when it discovered in a vault the silverware from Abraham Lincoln's fu-

neral car, which it had purchased decades earlier. The museum has recently been refurbished. Its displays cover the history of UP; exhibits include a re-creation of Lincoln's funeral car, artifacts from the driving of the Golden Spike, a model of a centralized traffic control panel, and an O scale model railroad. The museum is in UP's general office building at 1416 Dodge Street in downtown Omaha.

Locomotives	2 steam, 1 motor car
Cars	Open cars
Displays	4 locomotives, 1 motor car, numerous freight and passenger cars
Dates open	May 22-November 1, Friday, Saturday, Sunday, and holidays, 8:30 a.m.-4:30 p.m.
Admission	Free
Memberships	Write for information.
Special events	Steam-ups — Memorial Day, July 4, Labor Day, and Nevada Day
Nearby attractions	Lake Tahoe, Virginia City, Virginia & Truckee Railroad
Address	2180 South Carson Street, Carson City, NV 89710
Phone	(702) 885-5168 (during season); 885-4810 (year-round)

NEVADA STATE RAILROAD MUSEUM

The Virginia & Truckee Railroad was built to serve the gold and silver mines of Virginia City, Nevada. The mines were played out by 1900, and the V&T hung on until 1950, occasionally selling an antique locomotive or car to a Hollywood movie studio. It was the archetypal western short line — not much mileage, not much business, not much income. When the movie studios hit hard times, the state of Nevada bought back some of the V&T's equipment, then more of it. A museum was established at Carson City, the state capital; it opened May 31, 1980, 30 years to the day after the V&T made its last run. The locomotives are steamed up on special occasions, and there are plans to build track to operate them at Carson City. The museum is on U. S. 395 south of downtown Carson City. There are restaurants and motels in Carson City.

Displays	4-6-0 No. 40, being prepared for operation; numerous freight, passenger, and maintenance of way cars
Dates open	Weekends 10 a.m.-6 p.m.; Monday-Friday 8-10 and 3-6
Admission	Free; donations are welcome
Memberships	Write to Friends of the Nevada Northern Railway, Box 608, Ely, NV 89301.
Special events	Railfair — Saturday and Sunday of Memorial Day weekend
Nearby attractions	Lehman Caves National Monument, ghost towns, and areas for picnics, camping, fishing, and hunting
Address	P. O. Box 40, East Ely, NV 89315
Phone	(702) 289-2085

NEVADA NORTHERN RAILWAY MUSEUM

The Nevada Northern Railway was completed in 1906 from Ely, Nevada, north to a connection with the Southern Pacific at Cobre. The principal reason for the road's existence was the copper mine at Ely. When the mine and smelter shut down in 1983 the railroad ceased operation; the railroad's owner, Kennecott Copper Corp., donated the East Ely station and several pieces of rolling stock to the city of Ely and the White Pine Historical Railroad Foundation to form the nucleus of a railroad museum. Among the rolling stock was 4-6-0 No. 40 — when the Nevada Northern replaced its passenger train with a bus in 1941 it carefully preserved the steam locomotive and the two cars, bringing them out from time to time for excursions.

The museum is in the East Ely depot at East 11th Street and Avenue A; it includes NN's shops, which have changed little since the railroad began operation. The museum is still in its early stages: Train operations, a snack bar, and a picnic area are in the plans. Access for the handicapped is somewhat limited. Ely is at the junction of U. S. Routes 6, 50, and 93 in east-central Nevada. Lodging and food are available in Ely. The nearest cities are Reno, Las Vegas, and Salt Lake City, all 250-300 miles away.

Locomotives	2 steam
Cars	Gondolas, caboose
Displays	Freight and passenger cars; shop is open to view
Schedule	Memorial Day–September, daily, every 40-45 minutes from 10:30 a.m. to 5:20 p.m.; additional trip at 6 mid-June to Labor Day. Charter trips available.
Fares	Adults $2.75, children 5-12 $1.50 (under 5 free), all-day pass $6. Group discounts available. Checks accepted.
Nearby attractions	Mine tours, historic mansion tours, Nevada State Railroad Museum, Reno, Lake Tahoe
Address	P. O. Box 467, Virginia City, NV 89440
Phone	(702) 847-0380

VIRGINIA & TRUCKEE RAILROAD

The Virginia & Truckee Railroad ceased operation on May 31, 1950; its line to Virginia City had been abandoned in 1939. In the mid-1970s a mile and a half of track was restored from Virginia City through a tunnel to Gold Hill, and an excursion train began operation through the heart of the Comstock Lode mining area.

The station (actually a coach, standing in for a station building) is on F Street south of Washington Street in Virginia City. There is a parking lot on the east side of F Street. Tickets can also be purchased at V&T Car 13, which is on C Street opposite the post office. Several freight and passenger cars are on display. Cab rides can be arranged for adults with some knowledge of railroads. Soft drinks are available on the train. Staff are on premises year round. Food and lodging are available in Virginia City; Reno and Carson City are about a half-hour away.

Locomotives	2 steam (1 Climax, 1 Heisler)
Cars	Open excursion cars
Displays	1930 Reo rail bus, small switch engine
Dates open	Weekends Memorial Day through June, daily in July and August, weekends to mid-October, 10 a.m.-5 p.m. Admission includes train ride.
Schedule	Steam train operation begins July 1. Charter trips available.
Admission	Adults $5, children 6-12 $4 (under 6 free)
Nearby attractions	Loon Mountain, Lost River, White Mountains, Mount Washington Cog Railway, Conway Scenic Railroad
Address	Box 1, Lincoln, NH 03251
Phone	(603) 745-8913

WHITE MOUNTAIN CENTRAL RAILROAD

At Clark's Trading Post in Lincoln, New Hampshire, two geared steam locomotives operate passenger trains on the White Mountain Central, 1¼ miles of track along the Pemigewasset River and through a covered bridge. Other attractions at Clark's include an ice cream parlor, a maple syrup shop, performing bears, and numerous other tourist attractions. Staff are on premises year-round. Clark's Trading Post is on U. S. 3 at Exit 33 of I-93. Lincoln is about 65 miles north of Concord and 25 miles south of Littleton. Food and lodging are available in Lincoln.

Locomotives	2 diesel
Cars	Coaches
Displays	Cabooses, milk car, baggage car
Schedule	End of June to Labor Day, daily, leave Meredith 9:30 a.m., 11:30 a.m., 1:30 p.m., and 3:30 p.m., stop in Weirs on the hour 10-5. Late May to late June and Labor Day to mid-September, weekends, leave Meredith 10:30, 12:30, and 2:30, stop in Weirs on the hour 11-4. July and August, Thursday, Friday, and Saturday leave Meredith 6:45 p.m., Weirs 7, Laconia 7:30 for Lochmere and return. Mid-September to mid-October, weekends, leave Meredith for Weirs and Lakeport 9:30, 12:45, and 3:45; leave Meredith for Plymouth 11:15 and 2:15. Charter trips available.
Fares	Meredith-Lakeport, boarding at either Meredith or Weirs Beach: adults $6, children 5-12 $4 (under 4 free). Weirs-Meredith and Weirs-Lakeport, $5/$3. Meredith-Plymouth or Weirs-Plymouth, $7/$5. Meredith-Weirs-Lakeport-Plymouth, $11/$8. Meredith-Weirs-Lochmere, $7/$5. Laconia-Lochmere, $5/$3. Group discount available.
Nearby attractions	Lake Winnipesaukee, White Mountains

Address	P. O. Box 6268, Lakeport, NH 03246
Phone	(603) 528-2330

WINNIPESAUKEE RAILROAD

The Winnipesaukee Railroad operates excursion trains over former Boston & Maine track between Lochmere and Plymouth, in the lake region of central New Hampshire. (Freight service is operated on the same rails by the New England Southern.) The basic pattern of operation is round trips from Meredith south along the shores of Meredith Bay and Paugus Bay to Lakeport, 9 miles, stopping at Weirs Beach in both directions. In July and August an evening trip (the *Sunset Special*) runs another 7 miles beyond Lakeport along Lake Winnisquam and Silver Lake to Lochmere, stopping at Weirs and Laconia. During the fall foliage season Meredith-Lakeport trips alternate with trips from Meredith north to Plymouth, 13 miles — reservations are recommended for those trips. Passengers may board at Meredith or Weirs Beach. Free parking is provided only at Meredith. Refreshments are available there; food and lodging can be found throughout the area.

Meredith

Locomotives	8 steam
Cars	Coaches
Displays	*Old Peppersass*, world's first cog railway locomotive
Schedule	Mid-May to mid-October, daily, hourly departures from 10 a.m. (8 a.m. mid-June to Labor Day) and hourly as needed until 3 hours before sunset. Charter trips available.
Fares	$25 round trip to summit for persons age 8 and over (children under 8 held on laps are free). Shuttle trip at Base Station $3. Credit cards accepted. Discounts available for groups of 20 or more with pre-season reservation.
Nearby attractions	White Mountains, Conway Scenic Railroad
Address	Summer, Mt. Washington, NH 03589; winter, P. O. Box 932, Littleton, NH 03561
Phone	Summer, (603) 846-5404; winter, (603) 444-6622

P &. ⊼ 🎁 ▣

Bob Hayden

MT. WASHINGTON COG RAILWAY

The Mt. Washington Cog Railway opened in 1869, the first mountain-climbing cog railroad in the world. It climbs to the summit of Mt. Washington, highest peak in the Northeast (6288 feet) with an average grade of 25 percent — 1 foot up for every 4 feet forward. During the 3¼-mile trip the train climbs 3760 feet. On a clear day the view from the top encompasses all six New England states. Only steam locomotives are used; most were built in the late 1800s and early 1900s, but the two newest ones date from 1972 and 1983. Trains operate from Base Station, east of U. S. 302 about halfway between North Conway and Littleton. There is a restaurant at the base and a snack bar at the summit. Food and lodging are available throughout the area. The trip to the summit and back takes about 3 hours. Train operations depend on weather conditions. The weather at the summit is never warm; take a jacket or a sweater.

Locomotives	2 steam, 3 diesel
Cars	Coaches, extra-fare parlor-observation
Displays	Maine Central 2-8-0, roundhouse, turntable, freight and passenger cars
Schedule	First Saturday in June through third Sunday in October, daily; also weekends and holidays in May and Thanksgiving weekend: leave North Conway 11 a.m. and 1, 2:30, and 4 p.m.; also 7 p.m. on Tuesday, Wednesday, Thursday, and Saturday in July and August. Charter trips available.
Fares	Adults $5, children 4-12 $3 (under 4 free). Group discounts available.
Special events	Railfan's Day (second Saturday after Labor Day)
Nearby attractions	Mt. Washington Cog Railway, White Mountains
Address	P. O. Box 947, North Conway, NH 03860
Phone	(603) 356-5251

CONWAY SCENIC RAILROAD

The railroad line that eventually became the Conway Railroad reached the village of North Conway, New Hampshire, in 1872 under the banner of the Portsmouth, Great Falls & Conway Railroad. The village was a growing summer resort, and the railroad erected there a large, ornate wooden depot. The PGF&C became part of the Eastern Railroad in 1878, and the Eastern was absorbed by the Boston & Maine in 1890. B&M's Conway Branch fared better than most other branch lines. North Conway developed into a winter sports area in the 1930s and passenger traffic increased, but in December 1961 the last passenger train left North Conway, and freight service ended in October 1972.

After long negotiations Boston & Maine sold the North Conway property, including the depot, and 7½ miles of track to three men who formed the Conway Scenic Railroad. Operation began in August 1974. Conway Scenic's trains operate on 5½ miles of track between North Conway and Conway, traversing farmland and offering views north to Mt. Washington and south to Mt. Chocorua. The round trip takes about 55 minutes. Food and lodging are available in North Conway, a resort town; the station is at the center of town. Staff are on the premises year-round. North Conway is about 140 miles north of Boston and 60 miles northwest of Portland, Maine.

North Conway   **NEW HAMPSHIRE-99**

Locomotives	3 steam, 4 diesel
Cars	Open-platform coach, excursion flat car, caboose
Displays	Assorted locomotives and cars not in service or awaiting restoration
Schedule	Palm Sunday through mid-October, weekends, noon-5 p.m.; July and August, daily, noon-5. Trains operate every 30 minutes. Steam locomotives are used only on weekends.
Admission	State Park, $2 per car Memorial Day-Labor Day
Fares	$1 (children under 3 free). In-state checks accepted.
Memberships	Write for information.
Special events	Andrews Raid re-enactment on Fathers' Day, Santa Claus Special first three weekends in December
Nearby attractions	Beaches
Address	P. O. Box 622, Farmingdale, NJ 07727-0622
Phone	(201) 938-5524

William J. Husa Jr.

NEW JERSEY MUSEUM OF TRANSPORTATION

The Pine Creek Railroad of the New Jersey Museum of Transportation is a 3-foot-gauge line at Allaire State Park. Trains operate over a ¾-mile loop of track and offer a 1½-mile, 10-minute ride through woods and fields. The state park includes Historic Howell Works, a restored iron mining community of the early 1800s. Farmingdale is west of Asbury Park and southeast of Freehold. To reach Allaire State Park, take Exit 31 (Route 547, about halfway between U. S. 9 and the Garden State Parkway) from I-195; then go north a short distance to Route 524. The park contains a restaurant and a snack bar; food and lodging are available in Freehold, Lakewood, Belmar, and Manasquan.

Locomotives	1 steam, 4 diesel, 1 gas-electric car
Cars	Ex-Lackawanna and Central of New Jersey coaches
Displays	0-6-0T, Mack locomotive, caboose, several private cars
Schedule	Weekends and holidays, mid-April through November, leave Ringoes 10:45 a.m. and 12:15, 1:45, 3:15, and 4:45 p.m. for Flemington, leave Flemington 45 minutes later; Sundays, July-October, leave Ringoes 12:15, 1:45, 3:15 and 4:45 for Lambertville; Tuesday-Friday, July and August, leave Ringoes 12:30, 1:30, 2:30, and 3:30, leave Flemington 30 minutes later. Charter trips available.
Fares	Adults $6, children 5-12 $3, children 3-4 $1. Checks and credit cards accepted. Group discounts available.
Nearby attractions	Delaware & Raritan Canal State Park, Washington Crossing State Park, outlet stores in Flemington
Address	P. O. Box 200, Ringoes, NJ 08551
Phone	(201) 782-9600

P ☕ 🅿 🎁 ▣

Bruce Russell

BLACK RIVER & WESTERN RAILROAD

The Black River & Western was incorporated in 1961. In 1965 it leased a portion of the Pennsylvania Railroad's Flemington Branch from Flemington to Ringoes, New Jersey, and began excursion service, and in 1970 it acquired the rest of the branch from Ringoes to Lambertville and began operating freight service. In 1976 the BR&W expanded again by acquiring Central of New Jersey track between Flemington and Three Bridges. The primary route for BR&W's passenger trains is between Ringoes and Flemington, 6 miles north. On summer Sundays trains also operate between Ringoes and Lambertville, 7 miles southwest on the Delaware River. Charter trips can be operated to Three Bridges. The road's roster includes four diesels (an RS1, a T6, and two CF7s) used in year-round freight service, ex-Great Western 2-8-0 No. 60, and former Pennsylvania Railroad gas-electric car 4666. Restaurants and lodging can be found in Flemington; there are also restaurants in Lambertville.

Displays	Bangor & Aroostook F3s, numerous ca- booses, large Lionel layout, railroadiana
Dates open	April-October, noon-4 p.m. Sundays
Admission	Free, donations welcome
Memberships	Write for information.
Special events	Railroad Festival — last Saturday of October
Nearby attractions	Morris Museum, General Washington's Headquarters in Morristown
Address	P. O. Box 16, Whippany, NJ 07981

WHIPPANY RAILWAY MUSEUM

The Whippany Railway Museum was chartered in 1973. In 1985 it acquired its present name and moved to new quarters in the former freight house of the Morristown & Erie Railway at Whippany, New Jersey. The building contains a gift shop, a collection of railroadiana, and a Lionel train layout. Nearby are approximately a dozen pieces of rolling stock owned by museum members and other railroad asso-ciations. The museum is at Route 10 and Whippany Road. To reach the museum by car, take Exit 35 (Route 10 East) from I-287 about halfway between Morristown and I-80. It is also accessible by bus or taxi from the NJ Transit commuter rail station in Morristown — the distance is about 2 miles. There are restaurants in Whippany and restaurants and lodging in Morristown.

Locomotives	4 steam, 1 diesel (used for switching)
Cars	Box cars rebuilt into passenger cars, snack and souvenir car, open observation car
Schedule	Mid-June to mid-October: leave Chama 10:30 a.m., return 4:30 p.m.; leave Antonito 10, return at 5. Charter trips available.
Fares	Round trip to Osier from either Chama or Antonito: adults $27, children under 12 $10; through trip with return by van: adults $41.50, children $20; overnight trip, adults $121, children $55. Checks and credit cards accepted.
Memberships	Write to Railroad Club of New Mexico, c/o Bill Lock, 5400 Phoenix N. E., Albuquerque, NM 87110.
Nearby attractions	Great Sand Dunes, Rio Grande National Forest, Carson National Forest, Jicarilla Apache Reservation
Address	P. O. Box 789, Chama, NM 87520
Phone	(505) 756-2151

CUMBRES & TOLTEC SCENIC RAILROAD

When the Denver & Rio Grande Western abandoned its 3-foot-gauge line between Antonito and Durango, Colorado, in 1968, the states of New Mexico and Colorado purchased a 64-mile segment of the line between Antonito and Chama, N. Mex., and the locomotives and cars necessary to operate the line. The line is now operated by Kyle Railways for the two states. It is the longest and highest narrow gauge steam railroad in the U. S.

Trains leave both terminals and meet at Osier, Colo., where passengers eat lunch (snacks are available on the train) and the trains exchange engines. Passengers then reboard and return to their starting points. The line from Chama (elevation, 7863 feet) climbs a 4 percent grade to the summit at Cumbres (10,015 feet) and descends to Osier (9634 feet). The climb from Antonito (7888 feet) to Osier is an easier one, averaging 1.4 per cent; the scenery includes Toltec Gorge, two tunnels, and enough sharp curves that the line crosses the Colorado-New Mexico boundary ten times.

Reservations are advisable; they are necessary for overnight trips. They can be made through travel agencies and AAA offices. Passengers can ride either half of the line or they can go all the way and return by van. Take a jacket or sweater — the weather can change quickly in the Rockies. Access for the handicapped is somewhat limited; persons with respiratory problems should consider the altitude. Chama is 106 miles northwest of Santa Fe on U. S. 64 and 84; Antonito is 110 miles north of Santa Fe and 30 miles south of Alamosa on U. S. 285. Food and lodging are available in Chama and Antonito.

Locomotives	2 steam, 2 diesel
Cars	Coaches, gondola car
Displays	New York, Ontario & Western private car used by President Grover Cleveland
Schedule	Weekends and holidays Memorial Day weekend through October; also Wednesday in July and August, departures at noon, 2, and 4 p.m. Charter trips available.
Fares	Adults $4, children 3-11 $2 (under 3 free). Group discounts available (reservations needed for groups).
Special events	Toy train show and sale in September
Nearby attractions	Canal Town, Letchworth State Park
Address	278 Main Street, Arcade, NY 14009
Phone	(716) 496-9877

ARCADE & ATTICA RAILROAD

Like several other railroads in this book, the Arcade & Attica is a common-carrier freight railroad that also runs excursion trains. Passenger trains run north from Arcade to Curriers, 7 miles, and back. The ride takes 1½ hours. Arcade is about 40 miles south-southeast of Buffalo, 3 miles east of Route 16. The Arcade & Attica station is on Routes 39 and 98 in downtown Arcade. Passengers should plan to be at the station a half hour before departure time. Soda, candy, and popcorn are available on the train. Restaurants and lodging can be found in Arcade.

Locomotives	2 diesel, 1 Brill motor car (nicknamed "The Red Heifer")
Cars	Coaches, open cars
Schedule	Late May-early November, weekends and holidays; late June-Labor Day, daily; leave Arkville for Highmount at 11 a.m. and 1 and 3 p.m. and to Halcottsville at noon, 2, and 4. Charter trips available.
Fares	Adults $5, children 5-11 (under 5 free), senior citizens $4.50. Discounts available for groups of 20 or more (reservations are needed for groups). Credit cards accepted.
Special events	Fiddlers Festival, Railroad Festival, train robberies
Nearby attractions	Auto Memories (Arkville), Hanford Mills Museum, Farmers Museum, Baseball Hall of Fame, Catskill Park
Address	P. O. Box 243, Stamford, NY 12167
Phone	(914) 586-3877; in New York 800-356-5615; in the rest of the Northeast 800-642-4443

DELAWARE & ULSTER RAIL RIDE

The Ulster & Delaware Railroad, a line from Kingston through the Catskills to Oneonta, New York, was purchased by the New York Central in 1932. It was abandoned in bits and pieces, and the last portion of the route was closed by Conrail in 1976. The Delaware & Ulster Rail Ride is one of three portions of the U&D remaining in service as tourist railroads (the other two are the Trolley Museum of New York at Kingston and the Catskill Mountain Railroad at Shokan). The Delaware & Ulster offers two 75-minute rides from Arkville, to Highmount, 6½ miles, and to Halcottsville, 6 miles, and return. The station is on Route 28 in Arkville, about halfway between Kingston and Oneonta. There is a snack bar in the station and a restaurant nearby; food and lodging can be found in Margaretville, 2 miles away. The station at Arkville has ramps to aid access for the handicapped.

Arkville

Displays	18 subway cars
Dates open	Monday-Friday except holidays, 10 a.m.-4 p.m.
Admission	Adults $1; children under 17, 50 cents
Nearby attractions	New York
Address	370 Jay Street, Brooklyn, NY 11201
Phone	(718) 330-3060

NEW YORK CITY TRANSIT EXHIBIT

The New York City Transit Authority maintains an exhibit of antique subway cars and memorabilia at its unused Court Street station, located at (or under) the corner of Boerum Place and Schermerhorn Street in Brooklyn. The authority has recently begun renovation and reconstruction of the exhibit. It will remain open during the work, but a phone call before you visit is advisable. The exhibit is not yet accessible to the handicapped because of steep stairs; for the same reason, the transit authority specifically cautions against wearing high heels. The nearest subway stations are Borough Hall in Brooklyn on the IRT 2, 3, 4, and 5 lines and Jay Street on the IND A and F lines.

Car	1 self-propelled railcar
Displays	8 streetcars and rapid transit cars
Dates open	Memorial Day-Columbus Day, weekends and holidays; July and August, daily, noon-5 p.m. Charter trips available.
Fares	Adults $1; children under 13, 50 cents. Group discounts available.

Memberships	Write for information.
Special events	Christmas run
Nearby attractions	Maritime Museum, Ulster & Delaware Rail Ride, Catskill Mountain Railroad
Address	89 East Strand, Kingston, NY 12401
Phone	(914) 331-3399

TROLLEY MUSEUM OF NEW YORK

The Trolley Museum of New York operates over 1½ miles of former Ulster & Delaware track at Kingston, N. Y. The scenery along the track is essentially urban: street running, waterfront industrial area, and the old U&D boat dock on the Hudson River. The only equipment in operation at the present time is a Brill Model 55 gasoline-powered railcar once on the roster of the New Haven Railroad.

Kingston is on the west shore of the Hudson River about 100 miles north of New York City and 50 miles south of Albany. To reach the museum, take Exit 19 of the New York State Thruway, then follow signs to downtown Kingston and the Urban Cultural Park on the waterfront. Food and lodging can be found in Kingston.

Locomotives	3 diesel, 2 gasoline
Cars	Flat cars
Displays	Steam locomotive, baggage car, coaches, cabooses
Schedule	Weekends and holidays Memorial Day-Columbus Day. Trains leave Mt. Pleasant hourly from 11 a.m. to 5 p.m. Charter trips available.
Fares	Adults $3 one way, $4 round trip; children 4-11 any ride $1 (under 4 free). Group discounts available. Checks accepted.
Memberships	Write for information.
Special events	Moonlight runs, hay rides, Christmas runs
Nearby attractions	Maritime Museum, Trolley Museum of New York, Catskills
Address	P. O. Box 46, Shokan, NY 12481
Phone	(914) 688-7400; for recorded information, 657-8233

CATSKILL MOUNTAIN RAILROAD

The Catskill Mountain Railroad operates over a 3-mile portion of the former Ulster & Delaware Railroad along Esopus Creek between Mt. Pleasant and Phoenicia, New York. The round-trip ride takes about 40 minutes. The usual motive power is a 35-ton diesel locomotive built by the Davenport Locomotive Works; passengers ride on open flat cars. There are restaurants in Phoenicia and lodging in Mt. Pleasant. Mt. Pleasant is 20 miles west of Kingston on Route 28.

Mt. Pleasant   **NEW YORK-107**

Locomotives	2 diesel
Cars	Vintage and modern coaches, dining car, open observation car
Displays	Bicycles, autos, horse-drawn vehicles, box car, railroad crane
Schedule	Weekends May-November, leave Flemingville noon and 1:30, 3, and 4:30 p.m., leave Newark Valley 12:45, 2:15, 3:45, and 5:15; Saturday only leave Flemingville 7 p.m. for North Harford, arrive Flemingville 10:30. Charter trips available.
Fares	11-mile trip: adults $4.50, children 6-12 $2.50 (under 6 free); Evening Express (42-mile trip): all ages $10. Group discounts available.
Memberships	Write for information.
Special events	Owego Strawberry Festival (late June), Newark Valley Depot Days (August 1-2), Berkshire Heritage Day (September 13), Newark Valley Apple Festival (October 10-11), Santa's Trains (December)
Nearby attractions	Corning Glass Works, Watkins Glen State Park, Finger Lakes region, wineries, speedway
Address	R. D. 4, Box 4240, Owego, NY 13827
Phone	(607) 642-5511

P &. A. 🎁 ▣ ⑪ TIOGA CENTRAL

TIOGA CENTRAL RAIL EXCURSIONS

The Tioga Central operates afternoon excursion trains over a former Lehigh Valley line from Flemingville (5 miles north of Owego, New York, on Route 38) to Newark Valley, 5½ miles, and a Saturday evening train from Flemingville to North Harford and return. Trains between Flemingville and Newark Valley stop on request at several intermediate points for passengers who want to visit parks and restaurants. The train fare includes admission to the Tioga Transportation Museum at Flemingville and the Newark Valley Depot Museum. The Saturday evening train includes a dining car. Reservations are required for dinner — phone the Mer Bleue restaurant, (607) 625-9917. There is a snack bar at the Flemingville depot. Food and lodging are available in Owego, just north of the Pennsylvania border 25 miles west of Binghamton.

Locomotives	Fairmont speeder	**Fares**	50 cents	
Cars	Open crew cars	**Memberships**	Write for information.	
Displays	Interurbans, streetcars, maintenance of way equipment, automobiles, buses	**Nearby attractions**	Oatka Depot Railroad Museum, Darian Lake Amusement Park, Genesee Country Village	
Dates open	Year-round, Sundays, 11 a.m.-5 p.m. Group tours available on weekdays by reservation.	**Address**	P. O. Box 136, West Henrietta, NY 14586	
Admission	Adults $1; children under 13, 50 cents. Group discounts available.	**Phone**	(716) 533-1112	

NEW YORK MUSEUM OF TRANSPORTATION

The New York Museum of Transportation is located on East River Road at Town Line Road in the town of Rush, about 15 minutes south of Rochester and 2 miles south of Exit 46 of the New York State Thruway. The museum building houses streetcars and interurbans from western New York, and numerous other items are under restoration, including a gasoline-powered switching locomotive that worked in the Rochester subway. Weather permitting, the museum offers track-car rides over 1½ miles of track. The track is being extended to the Oatka Depot Railroad Museum (see next entry) to enable visitors to see both museums without having to drive the 4 miles between them. If you visit the museum in cold weather, keep in mind that the visitor center is heated but the main building is not. Food and lodging are available in Henrietta, a suburb of Rochester, and throughout Rochester.

Displays	Diesel locomotives, freight and passenger cars	**Nearby attractions**	New York Museum of Transportation, Darian Lake Amusement Park, Genesee Country Village
Dates open	Memorial Day weekend-October, Sundays, 1-5 p.m.	**Address**	P. O. Box 664, Rochester, NY 14603
Admission	Free; donations welcome.	**Phone**	(716) 533-1431
Memberships	Rochester Chapter, NRHS; write for information.		

OATKA DEPOT RAILROAD MUSEUM

The Rochester Chapter of the National Railway Historical Society has a museum in a former Erie Railroad station (named Scottsville, Pixley, Oatka, and Industry at various times) 12 miles south of Rochester. It is located on Route 251 at 282 Rush-Scottsville Road. The museum's collection includes a Lehigh Valley RS3, an Eastman Kodak GE 80-ton switcher, and numerous freight and passenger cars. Rochester Chapter NRHS is cooperating with the New York Transportation Museum (see previous entry) to build a line between the two museums. There are restaurants in nearby Scottsville; food and lodging can be found throughout Rochester.

Dates open	May-October, Sundays, 2-5 p.m. Other times by appointment.
Admission	Free
Memberships	Central New York Chapter, NRHS; write for information.
Nearby attractions	Erie Canal exhibit, fish hatchery
Address	Box 229, Marcellus, NY 13108

MARTISCO STATION MUSEUM

When the Auburn & Syracuse Railroad was built in the 1830s it bypassed the village of Marcellus, 10 miles from Syracuse, but built a station about 2 miles away. The Auburn & Syracuse became part of the New York Central, and a short line was built (eventually the Marcellus & Otisco Lake Railway) to give Marcellus a rail connection. The NYC renamed its Marcellus station Martisco. The Central New York Chapter of the National Railway Historical Society purchased the Martisco station in 1966 to save it from demolition and has created a museum in the building. A former Pennsylvania Railroad dining car is parked next to the museum and contains the chapter's library. The chapter has 3 locomotives and 7 passenger cars on display at the New York State Fairgrounds; they are open only during the fair. The nearest restaurants are in Camillus; the nearest lodging is in Elbridge. Both are within a few minutes of the museum, and the city of Syracuse is about 10 miles away.

Locomotives	2 steam
Cars	Open cars, 1 coach
Dates open	May 23-October 25, 1987, 9 a.m.-6 p.m. Until the second Monday in June and after mid-August Monday-Friday hours are 9-5:30 and some park attraction are closed, but the train operates. Admission charge includes train ride.
Admission	Adults $9, children 4-12 $7, age 65 and over $8. Checks and credit cards accepted. Group discounts available (reservations needed for groups).
Special events	Old Timers Day
Nearby attractions	Mystery Hill, The Blowing Rock, Horn in the West (outdoor drama), Grandfather Mountain
Address	P. O. Box 388, Blowing Rock, NC 28605
Phone	(704) 264-9061

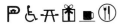

TWEETSIE RAILROAD

From 1918 to 1941 Boone, North Carolina, was the terminus of the 3-foot-gauge Linville River Railway, a subsidiary of the East Tennessee & Western North Carolina Railroad — nicknamed "Tweetsie." Ten-Wheeler No. 12 of the ET&WNC has been preserved to haul passengers around the Tweetsie Railroad theme park at Blowing Rock, N. C., 8 miles south of Boone on U. S. Routes 221 and 321.

Assisting the 4-6-0 is ex-White Pass & Yukon 2-8-2 No. 190, built in 1943. The train makes a 3-mile, 20-minute run around the perimeter of the park. The park includes a petting farm, live entertainment, kiddie rides, Indian village, gold mine, shops, and restaurants. Food and lodging can be found in Blowing Rock and Boone.

Blowing Rock

Historic Spencer Shops

Dates open	April-October, Monday-Saturday 9 a.m.-5 p.m., Sunday 1-5; November-March, Tuesday-Saturday 10-4, Sunday 1-4. Closed Thanksgiving, December 24, and Christmas.
Admission	Free; donations accepted
Memberships	$7.50-$1000. Write to North Carolina Transportation History Corporation Timekeepers, P. O. Box 44, Spencer, NC 28159.
Special events	Art shows, automobile shows, movies, Christmas exhibit
Nearby attractions	Waterworks Visual Arts Center, Grimes Mill, Hall House, Rowan Museum
Address	P. O. Box 165, Spencer, NC 28159
Phone	(704) 636-2889

SPENCER SHOPS STATE HISTORIC SITE

Spencer Shops was once the Southern Railway's primary repair facility. The railroad donated the buildings and site to the state in 1977 and 1979; they have become a transportation museum administered by the Division of Archives and History of the North Carolina Department of Cultural Resources. Exhibits range from prehistoric Indian canoes to airplanes. The railroad exhibits include several passenger and freight cars, among them James B. Duke's private car *Doris*. The museum is at 411 South Salisbury Avenue (U. S. Routes 29 and 70 and State Route 150) in Spencer, which is 2½ miles east of Salisbury. Southern's busy Washington-Atlanta main line passes to the south of the museum complex. Refreshments are available in the visitor center, and there is a restaurant across the street. Additional restaurants and lodging are available in Salisbury.

Displays	1 steam locomotive, 1 caboose
Dates open	Daily except Monday, 1-5 p.m.; other times by appointment
Admission	Free
Memberships	Individual $10, family $20, student $5; Wilmington Railroad Museum Foundation, P. O. Box 4674, Wilmington, NC 28406
Special events	Azalea Festival (early April), Wilmington River Fest (first week of October)
Nearby attractions	Beaches, battleship U. S. S. *North Carolina*
Address	501 Nutt Street, Wilmington, NC 28401
Phone	(919) 762-0858

P & ⊼ 🎁

WILMINGTON RAILROAD MUSEUM

The Wilmington Railroad Museum was dedicated on November 10, 1983. It is housed in the former Atlantic Coast Line freight office and warehouse, built in 1876, and oldest survivor of the group of buildings that once housed ACL's general offices. On display at the museum are ACL 4-6-0 No. 250, built in 1910; a steel caboose; and ACL artifacts. The building also houses the Cape Fear Model Railroad Club. The museum is at Red Cross and Water Streets in downtown Wilmington, about 12 blocks north of the bridge that carries U. S. 17, 74, and 76 over the Cape Fear River. Food and lodging are available within a block of the museum.

Wilmington　　　　　　　　　　**NORTH CAROLINA-113**

Displays	21 locomotives, freight cars, and passenger cars, including *Silver Dome*, the first dome car built in the U. S.
Dates open	Memorial Day-Labor Day, Wednesday-Sunday plus holidays, 1-5 p.m.; May and September, weekends 1-5; October, Sunday 1-5. Group tours available (reservations required).
Admission	Free, donations welcome
Memberships	Individual $10, family $12
Special events	Excursions and rail tours
Nearby attractions	Cedar Point, Seneca Caverns, Historic Lyme Village, Lake Erie Sorrowful Mother Shrine
Address	P. O. Box 42, Bellevue, OH 44811
Phone	(419) 483-2222

Robert McFaddin

MAD RIVER & NKP RAILROAD MUSEUM

The Mad River & NKP Railroad Society founded its museum in 1976, and it was adopted as a bicentennial project by the city of Bellevue that same year. The museum has grown to encompass a diverse collection of rolling stock, one that includes all the significant types of passenger cars without a great deal of duplication. Notable in the collection is *Silver Dome*, America's first dome car, converted by the Burlington from a coach in 1945. The museum is on State Route 269 just south of U. S. 20 in Bellevue. Restaurants and lodging can be found in Bellevue. The society occasionally sponsors excursion trains on mainline railroads; write for information about those trips.

Locomotives	1 diesel
Cars	Ex-Lackawanna coaches
Schedule	May-October, weekends and holidays, leave Mason noon, 2, and 4 p.m.
Fares	Adults $6; children under 13, $3. Checks and credit cards accepted. Group discounts available (reservations required for groups).
Nearby attractions	Kings Island, Football Hall of Fame, Jack Nicklaus Sports Center
Address	11020 Reading Road, Suite 501, Cincinnati, OH 45241
Phone	(513) 353-3533; 777-5777 for recorded information

P & 开 ◖▮

INDIANA & OHIO RAILROAD

The Indiana & Ohio operates freight trains on two routes, a former New York Central line from Valley Junction, Ohio, to Brookville, Indiana, and a former Pennsylvania Railroad line from Monroe to South Mason, Ohio. The I&O runs excursion trains between Mason and Lebanon, 8½ miles each way. The round trip takes 2 hours and traverses low rolling hills. Snacks are available on the train, and there are restaurants in Mason and Lebanon. Lodging can be found in Lebanon. Mason is about 25 miles northeast of Cincinnati on U. S. 42. The station is at Forest and Western Avenues in Mason.

Locomotives	1 steam, 2 diesel
Cars	Coaches
Schedule	Weekends Memorial Day through October and first three weekends of December, leave Nelsonville at noon for Diamond, at 2 p.m. for Logan. Charter trips available.
Fares	To Diamond, adults $4, children under 12 $3; to Logan, adults $7.50, children $4. Santa Trains are 50 cents more. Checks accepted. Group discounts available.
Memberships	Individual $10
Special events	Santa Trains (first three weekends in December)
Nearby attractions	Wayne National Forest, Hocking State Forest, Lake Hope, Burr Oak Lake
Address	P. O. Box 427, Nelsonville, OH 45764
Phone	(513) 335-0382

John B. Corns

HOCKING VALLEY SCENIC RAILWAY

The Hocking Valley Scenic Railway operates over a portion of the former Hocking Valley Railroad (it ran from Toledo to Athens and Gallipolis, Ohio, and became part of the Chesapeake & Ohio in 1930) between Nelsonville and Logan, Ohio. Trips are offered to Diamond (5 miles each way, 70 minutes round trip) and to Logan (12½ miles, 3 hours). The train is usually pulled by an ex-Lake Superior & Ishpeming 2-8-0. Reservations are advised for trips in October and the Santa Trains in December. Nelsonville is about 60 miles southeast of Columbus and 13 miles northwest of Athens on U. S. 33. The station is on Route 33 at Fulton Street. There are restaurants in Logan and Athens; lodging can be found in Nelsonville and Athens.

Locomotives	1 diesel
Cars	Coaches, gondola, caboose
Schedule	May-October, weekends and holidays, 1, 2:30, and 4 p.m. Santa Claus trains operate the first two weekends of December. Charter trips available.
Fares	Adults $3, children 3-11 $2 (under 3 free), age 62 and over $2.75. Checks and credit cards accepted. Discount for groups of 25 or more (50 cents off).
Memberships	Individual $10, family $25
Special events	Members' Day (July 4)
Nearby attractions	Heisey Glass Museum, Youth World Series Baseball, Newark Mounds (prehistoric area)
Address	P. O. Box 702, Newark, OH 43055
Phone	Weekdays (614) 345-9757; during operation and for recorded information 928-3827

P   ♿   ⛱   🎁

BUCKEYE CENTRAL SCENIC RAILROAD

One-hour train rides through fields and woods and along the Licking River are offered by the Buckeye Central. Trains operate from National Road station on U. S. 40 between Hebron and Jacksontown, Ohio, and run to Heath, 5 miles north, over a portion of a former Baltimore & Ohio branch. The station is about 40 miles east of Columbus. From the west use Exit 129 (Route 79) from I-70; go north a mile to U. S. 40, then east. From the east use Exit 131 (Route 13); go north to U. S. 40, then west. There are restaurants and lodging nearby.

Cars	20 streetcars and interurbans
Dates open	Memorial Day through September, Sundays and holidays 1-6 p.m.; June-August, Wednesday and Friday 10-3. Charters available mid-April through October (reservations required).
Admission	Adults $1.75, children 4-12 $1.25. Checks accepted.
Memberships	Regular $8, family $25
Special events	Moonlite Nites
Nearby attractions	Cleveland
Address	7100 Columbia Road, Olmsted Township, OH 44138
Phone	(216) 235-4725

P 木 🎁

TROLLEYVILLE, U. S. A.

In 1963 the Gerald E. Brookins Museum of Electric Railways — Trolleyville, U. S. A. — was established to formalize a collection of streetcars and interurbans that Brookins had acquired during the previous decade. Streetcars operate on a 2½-mile loop of track through a mobile home park. The ride takes about 30 minutes. The museum is about 14 miles southwest of downtown Cleveland on Columbia Road, State Route 252, north of Bagley Road and 10 minutes south of Exit 6 of I-480. Food and lodging are available in nearby Berea and North Olmsted.

Locomotives	2 diesel
Cars	Coaches, parlor car
Displays	2 steam switchers, Pullman, troop sleeper, freight cars
Schedule	Mid-May through October, weekends and holidays, leave Waterville 12:30 and 2:30 p.m., leave Grand Rapids 1:30 and 3:30; Memorial Day weekend-Labor Day, third departure from Waterville at 4:30, Grand Rapids at 5:30; July and August, Tuesday and Thursday, leave Waterville 10:30 and 1:30, leave Grand Rapids 11:30 and 2:30. Charter trips available
Fares	Adults $3.90 one way, $5.90 round trip; children 3-15 $1.95 one way, $2.95 round trip (under 3 free); age 65 and over $3.50 one way, $5.30 round trip. Parlor car 50 cents extra. Checks accepted. Group discounts available
Memberships	Write for information.
Special events	Dinner Train, May-October, first and third Saturdays of the month, leave Cloverleaf Station Restaurant (on U. S. 24 half a mile northeast of Grand Rapids) 7:45 p.m., earlier in September and October. Reservations required; phone (419) 832-2915.
Nearby attractions	Steamboat ride at Grand Rapids

Address P. O. Box 168, Waterville, OH 43566
Phone (419) 878-1177

TOLEDO, LAKE ERIE & WESTERN RAILWAY & MUSEUM

A few miles southwest of Toledo the Toledo, Lake Erie & Western runs excursion service over a 10-mile portion of the former Nickel Plate (before that, part of the Clover Leaf). Scenery along the way is primarily farmland. The route parallels the Maumee River and crosses it near Grand Rapids on a 900-foot-long bridge. Cars include coaches and an extra-fare parlor car with swiveling reclining seats. To reach the depot at Waterville, take Exit 4 from the Ohio Turnpike; then U. S. 20 East (south by the compass) 2 miles to U. S. 24; then 24 southwest to Waterville. From I-475 simply take the U. S. 24 exit. In Waterville turn right on Ohio Route 64; follow it three blocks to Sixth Street and turn right again on Sixth to the station. Although the trains are not easily accessible to the handicapped, the staff will assist as needed. There are soda machines at the depot and restaurants in Waterville and Grand Rapids. Lodging can be found in Maumee and Toledo.

Waterville

Cars	14 streetcars and interurbans
Displays	2 steam locomotives, gas-electric car, 5 passenger cars
Dates open	May 31-September 6, Sunday 1-5 p.m. Charters available.
Admission	Adults $2.50, children 4-12 $1.50, age 60 and over $1.50. Checks accepted. Group discounts available.
Memberships	Write for information.
Special events	Members' Day (fall)
Nearby attractions	Ohio Historical Society, Center of Science and Industry, Columbus Zoo, Wyandot Lake Amusement Park
Address	Box 171, Worthington, OH 43085
Phone	(614) 885-7345 during operation; 486-2265 year-round

OHIO RAILWAY MUSEUM

The Ohio Railway Museum was established in 1948 with a single interurban car, Ohio Public Service No. 21. It now has more than 30 pieces of railroad equipment and operates electric cars on 1½ miles of track laid on a portion of the roadbed of the Columbus, Delaware & Marion interurban line. The ride takes about 12 minutes. The museum is located at 990 Proprietors Road, just north of Ohio Route 161, in Worthington, a northern suburb of Columbus. From I-71, take the Worthington-New Albany exit, turn west, then north at the third traffic light. From U. S. 23 turn east on Route 161, then north at the second trafffic light. The museum has only a soda machine, but food and lodging can be found in Worthington.

Displays	Caboose, tank car, box car, large collection of lanterns
Dates open	By appointment
Admission	Free, donations welcome
Nearby attractions	Pawnee Bill Museum, Jim Thorpe Home and Museum
Address	P. O. Box 844, Cushing, OK 74023
Phone	(918) 225-1657

CIMARRON VALLEY RAILROAD MUSEUM

In 1969 the Santa Fe closed its station at Yale, Oklahoma. The Read family purchased the building and moved it to a new site in nearby Cushing. It now houses a large collection of railroad artifacts and an extensive library. In 1974 the Oklahoma Heritage Association gave the museum an award for its role in preserving Oklahoma's history. The museum is a family operation and is open only by appointment. It is located on South Kings Highway in Cushing, which is approximately equidistant from Tulsa and Oklahoma City. Food and lodging are available in Cushing.

Cushing

Locomotives	1 steam, 1 diesel
Cars	Air-conditioned coaches
Schedule	Mid-June to Labor Day, weekends, leave Cottage Grove 10 a.m. and 2 p.m. with steam power; Monday-Friday, 2 p.m. only with diesel. Charter trips available.
Fares	Adults $7.50, children 2-11 $3.75, age 65 and over $6.75. Checks and credit cards accepted. Group discounts available.
Nearby attractions	Cascade Mountains
Address	P. O. Box 565, Cottage Grove, OR 97424
Phone	(503) 942-3368

OREGON PACIFIC & EASTERN RAILWAY

The Oregon Pacific & Eastern extends from Cottage Grove, Oregon, 17½ miles into the Cascade Range. Its primary purpose is to carry out lumber and forest products, but during the summer it also carries passengers. Trains leave Cottage Grove daily at 2 p.m. for a 2-hour round trip. On weekends steam power is used instead of die-sel, and there is also a 10 a.m. trip. Snacks are available on the train. Reservations or arrival at the station 30-45 minutes before departure are advised for the weekend trips. The station is at The Village Green. Cottage Grove is 20 miles south of Eugene; food and lodging can be found there.

Displays	More than 20 streetcars and interurbans		available; reservations are required for groups.
Dates open	May-October, weekends and holidays 11 a.m.-5 p.m.; June-August, daily 11-5. Charters are available.	**Memberships**	Write for information.
		Nearby attractions	Wineries
Admission	Adults $3, children 5-17 $2, age 65 and over $2. Admission includes unlimited rides. Checks accepted. Group discounts	**Address**	17744 S. W. Ivy Glenn Drive, Beaverton, OR 97007
		Phone	(503) 642-5097 evenings only

TROLLEY PARK

The Oregon Electric Railway Historical Society operates a museum on roadbed that once served a logging railroad at Glenwood, Oregon, 38 miles west of Portland. The museum includes a 1¾-mile track on which trolleys operate, carbarn and shops, a gift shop and bookstore, and picnic, swimming, and overnight camping areas. To reach Trolley Park, take U. S. 26, the Sunset Highway, west from Portland to the junction with Oregon Route 6, the Wilson River Highway. Follow Route 6 12 miles west; the museum is near milepost 38. There are restaurants in Glenwood and lodging in Hillsboro, about 20 miles back toward Portland. Children visiting the museum must be accompanied by adults.

Locomotives	1 steam, 1 diesel, 1 gasoline	**Fares**	Train: adults $1.75, children 3-11 $1, age 65 and over $1. Group discounts available.
Cars	Semi-enclosed cars		
Dates open	Zoo: daily, opens at 9:30 a.m. Closing time depends on the season.	**Nearby attractions**	Forestry Center, Rose Garden, Japanese Garden
Schedule	Train: daily during the summer, weekends spring and fall, weather permitting. Charter trips available.	**Address**	4001 S. W. Canyon Road, Portland, OR 97221
Admission	Zoo: adults $2.50, children 3-11, age 65 and over $1	**Phone**	(503) 226-1561

WASHINGTON PARK ZOO RAILROAD

Portland's Washington Park Zoo has a 30″-gauge railroad on which trains powered by steam, diesel, and gasoline locomotives operate. From April through October trains run from the zoo to the Washington Park Rose Gardens and back, a half-hour, 4½-mile ride; during the rest of the year they operate only on the zoo grounds. The line includes a stretch of 6 percent grade. Train operations are subject to cancellation during rain. Restaurants and lodging can be found throughout Portland.

Glenwood   Portland

Displays	Pennsylvania Railroad GG1 electric locomotive, passenger cars, caboose, HO scale model railroad
Dates open	Year round Tuesday-Saturday 10 a.m.-5 p.m., Sunday 12:30-5; Memorial Day through September Monday 10-5
Admission	Adults $2.50, children under 12 $1, age 60 and over $1.75. Group discounts available.
Memberships	Write for information.
Nearby attractions	Horseshoe Curve, Fort Roberdeau, Bedford Village, Baker Mansion, Glendale Lake
Address	1300 Ninth Avenue, Altoona, PA 16602
Phone	(814) 946-0834

RAILROADERS MEMORIAL MUSEUM

Altoona, Pennsylvania, was where the Pennsylvania Railroad began its climb over the Alleghenies — a few miles west of the city is Horseshoe Curve, where the line doubled back on itself to gain altitude — and Altoona was the site of the Pennsy's principal shops. (Under Conrail's ownership the line is the busiest mountain railroad in the U. S. and the shops are still repairing diesels and freight cars.) The history of the Pennsylvania Railroad in Altoona is the central theme of the Railroaders Memorial Museum. Displays include numerous pieces of PRR rolling stock, artifacts, and memorabilia. The museum is located at the end of Station Mall, on Ninth Avenue three blocks northeast of 17th Street. To get to the museum, follow U. S. 220 into Altoona from the north or south, then turn northwest onto 17th Street. Follow 17th to Ninth Avenue, and turn right on Ninth. There are restaurants in the adjacent mall; lodging can be found in Altoona. To reach Horseshoe Curve from the museum, follow 17th Street northwest to Broad Avenue, Broad southwest to 40th Street, then 40th west several miles.

Locomotives	2 steam	Mine: Adults $3.50; children $1.50. Discounts available for groups of 10 or more (reservations required).
Cars	Rebuilt mine cars, caboose	
Dates open	Memorial Day-Labor Day, daily 10 a.m.-6 p.m.; May, September, and October, weekends 10-6	**Nearby attractions** Ashland Anthracite Museum, Knobles Grove
Fares	Train: adults $1.50; children under 12, 75 cents	**Address** 19th and Oak Street, Ashland, PA 17921 **Phone** (717) 875-3850

ASHLAND COMMUNITY ENTERPRISES

The Pioneer Tunnel Coal Mine at Ashland has become a museum of anthracite mining. Tours of the museum are conducted with battery locomotives and open mine cars. In conjunction with the tunnel tour, a steam-powered 42"-gauge train takes visitors on a tour of a strip-mining area. The ¾-mile train ride around the side of Mahanoy Mountain takes about 30 minutes; the coal mine tour takes 35 minutes. Jackets or sweaters are recommended for the mine tour. Ashland is located about halfway between Harrisburg and Wilkes-Barre and about halfway between Reading and Williamsport. It is on Route 61 approximately 8 miles west of the Frackville exit of I-81. There are motels and restaurants in Ashland.

Locomotives	2 steam, 2 diesel (steam power is normally used only on weekends)	tions are required for the Mt. Holly Springs trips. Charter trips available.
Cars	Coaches, double-deck open car; plus food service car on the Mt. Holly Springs trains	**Fares** Biglerville: Adults $4.50, children 3-12 $3 (under 3 free); Mt. Holly Springs: adults $12, children $8. Group discounts available.
Schedule	To Biglerville: June-October, weekends 1 and 3 p.m.; July and August, Monday-Friday 11 and 1. To Mt. Holly Springs: Second Saturday of July, August, and September, first three Saturdays of October, and second Sunday in October, 10 a.m. Reserva-	**Special events** Raid by Confederate soldiers third Saturday in September (fares 25 cents higher) **Nearby attractions** Gettysburg National Military Park **Address** P. O. Box 745, Gettysburg, PA 17325 **Phone** (717) 334-6932

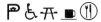

GETTYSBURG RAILROAD

The Gettysburg Railroad operates freight and excursion service on a former Reading branch line between Gettysburg and Mt. Holly Springs, Pennsylvania. Two excursions are offered: round trips from Gettysburg to Biglerville, 8 miles each way, and Gettysburg to Mt. Holly Springs, 25 miles each way. The latter trip is offered only seven times each year; reservations are required, and that train carries a food service car. The Gettysburg depot is on Constitution Avenue just off North Washington Street, one block north and one block west of Lincoln Square at the center of Gettysburg. Food and lodging are available in Gettysburg.

Locomotives	1 diesel (ex-Bangor & Aroostook BL2)
Cars	Coaches
Displays	Replicas of *Stourbridge Lion* and gravity coach
Schedule	July 18 and 25, leave Honesdale 10 a.m. and 3 p.m.; July 19 and 26, leave Honesdale noon; October 3, 4, 10, 11, 17, and 18, leave Honesdale 9:30 and 2:30. Reservations are required. Charter trips available.
Fares	Honesdale-Lackawaxen: adults $10, children 3-11 $5, age 60 and over $9. Group discounts available. Checks and credit cards accepted.
Nearby attractions	Pocono Mountains, Delaware State Forest
Address	742 Main Street, Honesdale, PA 18431
Phone	(717) 253-1960

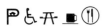

STOURBRIDGE LINE RAIL EXCURSIONS

In July and October the Wayne County Chamber of Commerce operates excursions between Honesdale and Lackawaxen, Pennsylvania, 25 miles, over the rails of the Lackawaxen & Stourbridge, a former Erie Railroad branch that is now part of the Delaware Otsego System. The usual power for the train is a rare and unusual diesel, a BL2, designed for branchline service by Electro-Motive. The route follows the Lackawaxen River, and the round trip takes 4½ hours. Sightseeing and food are available during the layover at Lackawaxen, and refreshments are available on board the train. Children under 12 must be accompanied by adults. Restaurants and lodging can be found in Honesdale, about 30 miles northeast of Scranton on U. S. Route 6.

Locomotives	1 steam
Cars	Coaches
Displays	Several restored cabooses
Schedule	Memorial Day weekend-Labor Day, weekends and holidays, also Sundays in September, leave Jim Thorpe at 1, 2, 3, and 4 p.m. October Saturdays, leave 1:30; October Sundays, leave 9:30 and 1:30. Reservations are required for trips in October. Charter trips available.
Fares	May-September (8-mile round trips): adults $3, children 6-11 $3 (under 6 free). October (foliage specials): adults $10, children $6. Checks accepted. Group discounts available.
Special events	Autumn Leaf Specials, Santa Claus Specials
Nearby attractions	Asa Packer Mansion, Flagstaff Park
Address	P. O. Box 285, Jim Thorpe, PA 18229
Phone	(717) 325-4606

RAIL TOURS, INC.

Rail Tours, Inc., operates two series of excursions out of Jim Thorpe (ex-Mauch Chunk), Pennsylvania, on a former Central Railroad of New Jersey branch. From the end of May through September trains operate to Nesquehoning, 4 miles; the round trip takes 40 minutes. Foliage specials in October run to Hauto, 8½ miles, and return; trips take 2¾ hours. The trains are usually pulled by a steam locomotive, former Canadian Pacific 4-6-0 No. 972. Refreshments are available on board. Trains leave from the former Jersey Central station on U. S. 209 opposite the Carbon County courthouse. Food and lodging are available in Jim Thorpe, about halfway between Allentown and Wilkes-Barre.

Jim Thorpe

Locomotives	2 steam, 2 diesel
Cars	Coaches, gondola
Displays	Cabooses, business car, HO scale model railroad
Schedule	May-October, Saturdays, 1, 2, 3, and 4 p.m. (motor car in May, September and October); Sundays and holidays, 1, 2, 3, 4, and 5 p.m.; first two Sundays of November, 1:15, 2, 2:45, 3:30, 4:30 (motor car). Charter trips operated; individual cars can be chartered also.
Fares	Adults $2.50, children 2-12 $1.25. Discounts available for groups of 20 or more (reservations required).
Special events	Antique Car Show, Steam Tractor Show, Santa Claus Special
Nearby attractions	Crystal Cave, Hawk Mountain Bird Sanctuary, Roadside America
Address	P. O. Box 24, Kempton, PA 19529
Phone	(215) 756-6469

WANAMAKER, KEMPTON & SOUTHERN RAILROAD

The Wanamaker, Kempton & Southern operates excursion trains over a portion of a former Reading Company branch from Reading to Slatington, Pennsylvania. Steam-powered trips take about 40 minutes and cover 6 miles in all, 3 each way; on Saturdays except during June, July, and August a self-propelled car named "Berksy Trolley" makes a 35-minute round trip covering 9 miles of track. Passengers have the option of detraining at Furhrman's Grove for a picnic and boarding a later train. Trains leave from the Kempton station. Kempton is about 5 miles north of Krumsville and Lenhartsville exits from U. S. 22 and I-78; it's about 30 miles north of Reading. Food and lodging can be found in Reading and in the towns along I-78.

WEST SHORE RAILROAD

Locomotives	1 diesel
Cars	Ex-Lackawanna coaches
Schedule	May-October, Sundays and holidays, plus Wednesdays in July and August, leave Lewisburg for Vicksburg at 2 p.m., leave Lewisburg for Montandon at 3; two or three times a month leave Lewisburg at 2 for Mifflinburg instead of Vicksburg and Montandon. Santa Claus Specials are operated in December. Charter trips available.
Fares	Lewisburg to Mifflin: adults $4.75, children 3-11 $2. Credit cards accepted. Lewisburg to Vicksburg or Montandon: adults $2.75, children $1. Group discounts available.
Nearby attractions	Little League World Series, Buggy Museum
Address	R. D. 3, Box 155, Lewisburg, PA 17837
Phone	(717) 524-2900

WEST SHORE RAIL EXCURSIONS

The West Shore Railroad operates freight service over a former Pennsylvania branch from Montandon, Pa., across the Susquehanna River and through Lewisburg and Vicksburg to Mifflinburg, almost 12 miles. West Shore Rail Excursions operates passenger service on the same line, usually a Lewisburg-Vicksburg round trip followed by a Lewisburg-Montandon round trip. Two or three times a month a trip through Vicksburg to Mifflinburg and back is operated instead of the trips to Vicksburg and Montandon. In Lewisburg trains load at Route 45 and Fairground Road. Passengers should be there at least 15 minutes before train time. Lewisburg is on the Susquehanna River about 60 miles north of Harrisburg and 7 miles south of I-80. Restaurants and lodging are available in Lewisburg.

Lewisburg　　　　　　　　　　　　　　　　**PENNSYLVANIA-129**

Locomotives	1 steam, 1 diesel
Cars	Ex-Reading and Central of New Jersey coaches
Displays	2 steam locomotive, Baldwin diesel, baggage car, mail car, artifacts
Schedule	April-October, Saturdays and holidays, 1:30 and 3:30 p.m., Sundays 11:30, 1:30, and 3:30. Charter trips available.
Fares	Adults $5, children under 11 $3 (babies not occupying a seat free), age 65 and over $4.50. Group discounts available.
Memberships	Write for information.
Special events	Railfan Weekend (last weekend in October), Santa Claus Specials (first weekend in December, reservations required)
Nearby attractions	Mercer Museum, New Hope Mule Barge Co., Bucks County Playhouse, Nockamixon State Park, Washington Crossing State Park, Black River & Western Railroad
Address	P. O. Box 612, Huntingdon Valley, PA 19006
Phone	(215) 862-2707 for train information; 379-2169 year-round

Francis A. Odyniec

NEW HOPE STEAM RAILWAY

The New Hope Steam Railway operates excursion trains from New Hope to Buckingham Valley, Pennsylvania, 7 miles, and back over a former Reading branch line. Freight service is operated on the line by the New Hope & Ivyland Railroad. During the 1¾-hour ride the train goes through woods and fields and climbs the 2 percent grade of Solebury Mountain. Trains depart from a restored 1891-vintage depot in the center of New Hope, which is a tourist center on the Delaware River about 40 miles north-northeast of Philadelphia. There are restaurants within a block of the New Hope station, and lodging can be found in the town.

Displays	Heisler fireless steam locomotive, passenger and freight cars, railroadiana			
Dates open	May and September, weekends and holidays 1-5 p.m.; June-August, Wednesday-Sunday 1-5. Other times by appointment.	**Nearby attractions**		Festival (last weekend of September), Christmas at the Station (first weekend of December) Lake Erie beaches, U. S. Brig *Niagara*, Fort LeBoeuf
Admission	Free, donation welcome	**Address**		P. O. Box 571, North East, PA 16428-0571
Memberships	Write for information.	**Phone**		(814) 725-1911 when museum is open;
Special events	Official opening for the season (third weekend in May), Wine Country Harvest			825-2724 for recorded information and to leave messages

LAKE SHORE RAILWAY MUSEUM

The Lake Shore Railway Historical Society, a chapter of the National Railway Historical Society, maintains a museum in the former New York Central passenger and freight stations in North East, Pennsylvania. The museum is at Robinson and Wall Streets on the north side of Conrail's main line a couple of blocks south of U. S. 20 and west of Pennsylvania Route 89. Food and lodging are available in North East, which is on Lake Erie just west of the New York border. The society also maintains a small fleet of passenger cars used for mainline excursion service; write for information on those trips.

Locomotives	1 diesel			over $5. Checks accepted. Discounts available for groups of more than 20.
Cars	Coaches, Pullman, concession car			
Schedule	Friday, Saturday, and Sunday, leave Drake Well Park noon and 3:30 p.m.; leave Rynd Farm 1:30. Charter trips available.	**Memberships**		Write for information.
		Nearby attractions		Drake Well, Music Museum
		Address		P. O. Box 68, Oil City, PA 16301
		Phone		(814) 676-1733
Fares	Adults $6, children 3-12 $3, age 60 and			

OIL CREEK & TITUSVILLE RAILROAD

The Oil Creek & Titusville operates excursion trains through northwestern Pennsylvania's oil country — where in 1859 oil was first extracted from the ground by drilling — over a former Pennsylvania Railroad line. Passengers may board at either end of the route: Rynd Farm on Route 8 about 3 miles north of Oil City and Drake Well Park on the south side of Titusville east of Route 8. (The Drake Well Park site will be replaced soon with a station at 409 South Perry Street — Truck Route 8 — in Titusville.) The train ride is 13½ miles each way, and the round trip takes 2½ to 3 hours. Snacks are available on board the train. Reservations should be made and tickets should be purchased at least 10 days before your trip — enclose a stamped self-addressed envelope with your ticket request — and be at the boarding area 30 minutes before departure. A few tickets are available at the stations an hour before departure. Food and lodging can be found in Titusville and Oil City.

North East   Oil City   **PENNSYLVANIA-131**

Locomotives	3 steam, 1 gas-electric, 2 motor cars, 2 diesel
Cars	Wooden coaches, caboose
Displays	Roundhouse and shop
Schedule	July and August, daily, on the hour from 11 a.m. to 4 p.m.; June, September, and October, weekends, 11-4. Charter trips available.
Fares	Adults $5, children 5-12 $2.50. Checks accepted. Group discounts available (reservations required).
Special events	Fall Spectacular (second weekend of October)
Nearby attractions	Shade Gap Electric Railway (see next entry), Raystown Lake, Lincoln Caverns
Address	Rockhill Furnace, PA 17249
Phone	(814) 447-3011

P ♿ 🎋 🎁 ☕

Kalmbach Publishing Co: George Drury

EAST BROAD TOP RAILROAD

The East Broad Top Railroad was the last 3-foot-gauge common carrier in the U. S. east of the Mississippi River. Its principal business was carrying coal. It ceased operation in April 1956, and the locomotives and cars were stored on the property. In 1960 the railroad's owner, a scrap dealer, was asked if the line could be reactivated to help celebrate the bicentennial of the town of Orbisonia. The East Broad Top reopened in August 1960 as a tourist railroad — doing business in its original location with the same locomotives, cars, and shop and roundhouse facilities. Staff are on the premises year-round. The EBT offers a 50-minute round-trip ride over 5 miles of track north from Orbisonia. Food is available within two blocks of the station in Orbisonia; lodging can be found 15 miles north in Mt. Union. Orbisonia is on U. S 522 about 15 miles north of Exit 13 of the Pennsylvania Turnpike (from the east use Exit 14) and about 50 miles southeast of Altoona.

Cars	8 streetcars and interurbans
Displays	Electroliner-Liberty Liner, cars under restoration
Schedule	Memorial Day through October, weekends and holidays, every half hour from 11 a.m. to 4 p.m. Charter trips available.
Fares	$1.50 per person over age 5 for unlimited rides on day of purchase, maximum of $5 per family. Group rates, $1.25 per person, $3 for "run-everything" plan.
Memberships	Sustaining $15, associate $8
Nearby attractions	East Broad Top Railroad, Raystown Lake, Lincoln Caverns
Address	Railways to Yesterday, Inc., P. O. Box 1601, Allentown, PA 18105
Phone	(814) 447-9576

SHADE GAP ELECTRIC RAILWAY

In 1963 a mile of standard gauge track was laid on the roadbed of the East Broad Top's Shade Gap Branch (see previous entry) by Railways to Yesterday. Trolleys run every half hour from a station across the tracks from East Broad Top's Orbisonia station; the ride takes about 25 minutes. The Shade Gap Electric Railway includes a museum with an exhibit of photographs depicting the history of Pennsylvania's electric railways. The trolley ride is not readily accessible to the handicapped, but the staff will assist as necessary. Children must be accompanied by adults. For notes on food and lodging, see the previous entry (East Broad Top).

Orbisonia   **PENNSYLVANIA-133**

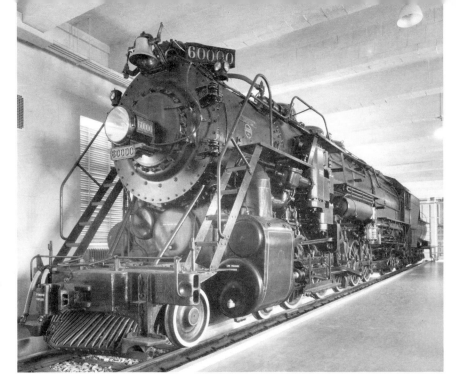

Displays	Baldwin 4-10-2 No. 60,000, 2 early steam locomotives, models
Dates open	Monday-Saturday, 10 a.m.-5 p.m.; Sunday, noon-5
Admission	Adults $4, children under 13 $3, age 65 and over $2.50. Group discounts available (reservations required).
Memberships	Write for information.
Nearby attractions	Independence Hall, Philadelphia Museum of Art
Address	20th Street and The Parkway, Philadelphia, PA 19103
Phone	(215) 448-1200; 564-3375 for recorded information

FRANKLIN INSTITUTE SCIENCE MUSEUM AND PLANETARIUM

Only a small part of the Franklin Institute's many exhibits are concerned with railroads; the museum collection comprises the larger subject of U. S. industrial growth, technology, and science. There are models, films and quizzes on video discs, and three full-size locomotives: a 4-4-0 built in 1842, Reading's *Rocket* of 1838, and Baldwin Locomotive Works No. 60,000, a 3-cylinder 4-10-2 built in 1926 and moved to the Franklin Institute in 1933. The Franklin Institute is at 20th Street and The Parkway in downtown Philadelphia, within walking distance of Suburban Station.

Cars	4 streetcars (1 from Philadelphia Rapid Transit, 3 from Red Arrow Lines)
Schedule	April through first weekend of December, weekends 11 a.m. till dusk; July-Labor Day, Thursday-Sunday, 11-dusk; Santa Claus Special second weekend of December. Charter trips available.
Fares	Adults $1; children under 13, 50 cents. Checks accepted. Group discounts available.
Memberships	Buckingham Valley Trolley Association; write for information.
Nearby attractions	Independence Hall, U. S. S. *Olympia*
Address	P. O. Box 7285, Philadelphia, PA 19101
Phone	(215) 627-0807

PENN'S LANDING TROLLEY

The Buckingham Valley Trolley Association, the Fidelity Bank, and the city of Philadelphia have teamed up to operate historic streetcars on a mile of track along the city's Delaware River waterfront. The 20-minute round trip passes historic neighborhoods such as Society Hill and Queen Village and offers views of a number of historic ships. The cars run on Delaware Avenue, five blocks east of Independence Hall. The north end of the run is at Race Street near the Ben Franklin Bridge; the south end is at Catherine Street. To reach the area from I-95, take the Tasker Street exit northbound or the Center City exit southbound. The 2nd Street station of the Market Street Subway is two blocks west of Delaware Avenue.

Locomotives	3 steam, 2 diesel
Cars	Ex-Lackawanna and Central of New Jersey coaches; business car and air-conditioned coach available for charter
Displays	8 steam locomotives, maintenance of way equipment
Schedule	May, except first week, Wednesday-Sunday plus Memorial Day; June, Thursday-Sunday; July and August, Tuesday-Sunday plus July 4; September, Thursday-Sunday plus Labor Day; October, Wednesday-Sunday plus Columbus Day: leave Scranton 11 a.m. and 1:30 p.m.; additional train at 3:45 p.m. weekends and holidays June-August and weekends in October. Charter trips available.
Fares	Adults $8.50, children 3-12 $5.50 (under 3 free), age 65 and over $7.50. Discount for groups of 25 or more (reservations required). Checks and credit cards accepted.
Memberships	Write for information.
Special events	Numerous events are offered; ask to be put on the mailing list.
Nearby attractions	Anthracite Museum, Everhart Museum, factory outlet shopping, Pocono Mountains

Address	P. O. Box 5250, Scranton, PA 18505-5250
Phone	(717) 969-1984; 969-1982 for recorded information

STEAMTOWN USA

Steamtown was established in 1963 by F. Nelson Blount, who had been acquiring steam locomotives for nearly a decade. By 1966 his collection was consolidated in Bellows Falls, Vermont, and excursion trains were operating over a portion of the defunct Rutland Railway. Blount was killed in a plane crash in 1967 but Steamtown continued to operate. In 1984 the collection was moved from Vermont to the former Lackawanna freight yards in downtown Scranton, Pennsylvania, and excursions began over a 13-mile portion of the ex-Lackawanna main line between Scranton and Moscow, Pa. The full collection is not yet on display but a representative sample can be viewed — all sizes up to and including Union Pacific Big Boy No. 4012, a 4-8-8-4. Trains depart from a platform near the former Lackawanna station, which has been converted to a Hilton hotel. Snacks are available on the train; restaurants and lodging can be found in Scranton. To reach Steamtown, use Exit 53 of I-81. In October 1986 Congress approved legislation adding Steamtown to the National Park System.

Locomotives	2 diesel
Cars	Ex-Reading coaches
Schedule	Memorial Day weekend through September, Sundays and holidays, leave Stewartstown 2 and 4 p.m.; October, Saturdays, 1 and 3, Sundays 11, 1, and 3. Charter trips available.
Fares	Adults $5, children 6-11 $3 (under 6 free). Checks and credit cards accepted. Discount of 10 percent for groups of 20 or more.
Special events	Midwinter, Easter, and Santa Claus trains
Nearby attractions	Strasburg, Pennsylvania Dutch country
Address	P. O. Box 155, Stewartstown, PA 17363
Phone	(717) 993-2936

Herbert H. Harwood Jr.

STEWARTSTOWN RAILROAD

The Stewartstown Railroad was opened in 1885 from Stewartstown, Pennsylvania, west 7½ miles to a connection at New Freedom with the Northern Central (later Pennsylvania, then Penn Central) line between Baltimore and Harrisburg. In 1972 floods damaged the PC line, and the Stewartstown ceased operations because its connection with the world was cut off. Eventually the commonwealth of Pennsylvania acquired the PC line and repaired it, and in January 1985 the Stewartstown resumed freight operations not only to North Freedom but all the way into York. Excursion trains began operating in July of that year. From May through September trains operate from Stewartstown to New Freedom; Fall Foliage Specials in October go only as far as Shrewsbury, 4 miles. Restaurants can be found in Stewartstown; the nearest lodging is in Glen Rock. Stewartstown is on Pennsylvania Route 851 about 4 miles east of I-83 and just north of the Maryland border. York is less than 20 miles away, and Harrisburg and Baltimore are each about 45 miles.

Strasburg, Pennsylvania, has more railroad museums and tourist railroads per square mile than any other place in North America. Within a mile or two of the intersection of Routes 741 and 896 are the Strasburg Rail Road, the Railroad Museum of Pennsylvania (those two are across the road from each other); the Choo-Choo Barn (a large operating Lionel layout), the Strasburg Train Shop (both just west of the Railroad Museum); the Toy Train Museum; and the Red Caboose Motel (sleep in cabooses, eat in dining cars). Strasburg is about 8 miles southeast of Lancaster in the heart of the Amish country. There are restaurants and motels throughout the area; some are within a mile of the Strasburg Railroad station. Advance reservations for lodging are advised during the tourist season.

Locomotives	6 steam, 1 diesel, 1 gasoline, 1 propane, 2 self-propelled railcars
Cars	26 assorted wood and steel coaches and open cars
Displays	The Railroad Museum of Pennsylvania is across the road.
Schedule	Third Saturday in March through April, weekends plus Good Friday and Easter Monday; May-October, daily; November, weekends and Thanksgiving Friday, and first two Saturdays and Sundays in December: noon, 1, 2, and 3 p.m. As spring and summer advance, trains are added at 11 a.m. and 10 a.m. except Sundays and at 4, 5, and 7 p.m., with extra trains on the half hour as needed; fall brings a tapering back to the noon, 1, 2, and 3 p.m. departures.
Fares	Adults $4.50, children 3-11 $2.50
Address	P. O. Box 96, Strasburg, PA 17579-0096
Phone	(717) 687-7522

Fred W. Schneider III

STRASBURG RAIL ROAD

The Strasburg Rail Road is the oldest railroad company in the U. S. operating under its original charter, and it was one of the first railroads to go after the tourist business in modern times. It was chartered in 1832 and operated until 1957, when storm damage caused a suspension of service. The line was purchased by a group of railroad enthusiasts who restored freight service and began running excursion trains in 1959. Trains run from the station at Strasburg 4½ miles through lush farmland and woods to a junction with Amtrak's Philadelphia-Harrisburg line (formerly Pennsylvania Railroad's main line) at Paradise (the railroads call it Leaman Place).

Kalmbach Publishing Co: George Drury

Locomotives	3 steam (2 on Strasburg Railroad)
Displays	65 cars and locomotives
Dates open	Monday-Saturday 9 a.m.-5 p.m., Sunday 11-5. Closed on some holidays.
Admission	Adults $2, children 6-17 $1; age 65 and over $1.50. Checks and credit cards accepted. Group discounts available.
Memberships	Friends of the Railroad Museum, c/o Tower View, P. O. Box 125, Strasburg, PA 17579
Address	P. O. Box 15, Strasburg, PA 17579
Phone	(717) 687-8628

P ♿ 🎁

RAILROAD MUSEUM OF PENNSYLVANIA

The Railroad Museum of Pennsylvania, operated by the Pennsylvania Historical and Museum Commission, is directly across the road from the Strasburg station. It has one of the largest collections of locomotives and cars in North America, with emphasis on rolling stock of the Pennsylvania Railroad. Many are inside the building, and many more are stored outside (the outdoor exhibit is open on weekends May through November). Two of the museum's Pennsylvania Railroad steam locomotives, 4-4-0 No. 1223 and 4-4-2 No. 7002, regularly operate on the Strasburg Rail Road. A third steam locomotive, a replica of Camden & Amboy's *John Bull*, operates at the museum on special occasions.

Displays	Toy trains, both static and operating
Dates open	April and November, weekends; also Good Friday, Easter Monday, Thanksgiving Friday, first two weekends of December, and Christmas week; May-October, daily, 10 a.m.-5 p.m.
Admission	Adults $1.75; children 7-12, 50 cents; age 65 and over $1.50. Credit cards accepted. Group discounts available.
Memberships	Train Collectors Association; write for information.
Address	P. O. Box 248, Strasburg, PA 17579
Phone	(717) 687-8976

MODEL RAILROADER: Jim Hediger

TOY TRAIN MUSEUM

The Train Collectors Association opened its national headquarters and museum building at Strasburg in 1977. The building contains displays of old toy trains bearing such famous brand names as Lionel and Ives and three large operating layouts. The museum is on Paradise Lane — from the Strasburg station drive east on Route 741 a short way, then turn left (north) onto Paradise Lane and go past the Red Caboose Motel.

Locomotives	2 steam
Cars	3 RDCs, ex-Lackawanna coaches
Displays	Cars and locomotives; display of photos in Temple station
Schedule	February, Sundays, noon and 2. March and April, weekends, leave Temple noon, 2 and 4 p.m. May, September, October, Friday, Saturday, and Sunday, noon, 2, and 4. Memorial Day-Labor Day, daily except Monday, also runs Monday holidays, 10, noon, 2, and 4. November and December until Christmas, Sundays, noon, 2, and 4. Charter trips available with either steam or the RDCs.
Fares	Adults $6, children 3-12 $4 (under 3 free), senior citizens $4 during May and September. Checks and credit cards accepted. Discounts available for groups of 25 or more (3 weeks' advance notice necessary).
Memberships	Annual passes are available; write for information.
Special events	Railfan Weekend (last weekend in June), special trains to King Frost Parade (last Saturday in October), Santa Specials (December 6, 13, and 20, 1987)
Nearby attractions	Wanamaker, Kempton & Southern; Roadside America; Crystal Cave.

Address	P. O. Box 307, Shoemakersville, PA 19555
Phone	(215) 562-4083

BLUE MOUNTAIN & READING RAILROAD

The Blue Mountain & Reading began operating freight service over a former Pennsylvania Railroad line between Temple and Hamburg, Pa., 13 miles, in September 1983, and on July 13, 1985, steam-powered passenger trains returned to the line. The railroad has two steam locomotives, ex-Gulf, Mobile & Northern 4-6-2 425 and ex-Reading 4-8-4 2101, and three Budd Rail Diesel Cars (RDCs), self-propelled stainless-steel coaches. The coaches and RDCs are heated, and the RDCs are air-conditioned. Trains make the 26-mile round trip in 1½ to 2 hours. The station in Temple, just north of Reading, is on Tuckerton Road between Routes 61 and U. S. 222. Passengers may also board in Hamburg 52 minutes after the times shown for Temple; the Hamburg station is on Route 61 at Station Road. Refreshments are available on the train. Food and lodging can be found in Temple, Reading, and Hamburg.

Cars	More than 20 streetcars
Dates open	May-September, weekends and holidays, noon-5 p.m.; July 4-Labor Day, daily, noon-5; October, Sundays, noon-5. Charters available.
Fares	Adults $2, children under 12 $1. Checks and credit cards accepted. Discounts available for groups of more than 25.
Memberships	Write for information.
Special events	Trolley Fair (last Sunday in June), County Fair (grounds adjacent to museum — second week of August)
Nearby attractions	Meadowcroft Village, covered bridges, harness racing
Address	Pennsylvania Railway Museum Association, P. O. Box 832, Pittsburgh, PA 15230
Phone	(412) 734-5780

ARDEN TROLLEY MUSEUM

The Arden Trolley Museum operates streetcars on a portion of the former Pittsburgh Railways right of way between Pittsburgh and Washington, Pennsylvania (the line still has regular trolley service from downtown Pittsburgh to Drake). The cars operated and displayed at the museum are primarily from streetcar and interurban lines of Pennsylvania, and the museum's unusual track gauge, 5′2½″, was used extensively in Pennsylvania. The museum is on the northern outskirts of Washington, about 25 miles southwest of Pittsburgh. Take Exit 8 (Meadowlands) from I-79 and follow the blue signs to the Arden Trolley Museum. Food and lodging are available in Washington and Meadowlands, each about 2 miles from the museum.

Locomotives	1 diesel
Cars	3 coaches, 1 caboose
Schedule	May, June, October-December, Sundays; July 4-Labor Day, daily; September after Labor Day, Wednesdays and Sundays: leave Newport 1:30 p.m., return 3:45. Charters available.
Fares	Adults $4, children under 14 $2.50, age 60 and over $3. Group discounts available. Checks accepted.
Memberships	National Railroad Foundation and Museum, P. O. Box 343, Newport, RI 02840. Individual $15, family $25
Special events	Easter Bunny Special
Nearby attractions	Historic Newport, International Tennis Hall of Fame
Address	P. O. Box 343, Newport, RI 02840
Phone	(401) 624-6951

OLD COLONY & NEWPORT RAILWAY

The Old Colony & Newport was chartered in 1863 to build a railroad from Newport, Rhode Island, to a connection with the Old Colony Railroad. Soon both names disappeared into the New Haven — but the name reappeared on a tourist railroad in 1978. The Old Colony & Newport carries excursionists north from Newport along the east shore of Narragansett Bay to Melville Marina and the Green Animals Topiary Gardens at Portsmouth, 8 miles. Admission to Green Animals is $3 for adults, $1.50 for children 6-11 with train ticket. After a 50-minute layover the train returns to Newport. The Newport station is downtown at America's Cup Avenue and Long Wharf. There are restaurants within a block of the station; lodging is available in Newport.

Newport

Locomotives	3 steam
Cars	Coaches, open cars
Schedule	Mid-June to late August, Monday-Saturday leave Hill City 8:15 and 10:30 a.m., leave Keystone Junction 9 and 11:30; daily leave Hill City 1 and 3:15 p.m., leave Keystone Junction 2 and 4 (no return trip from Hill City with the 4 o'clock departure).
Fares	Adults $12.50, children $8 (less than 42″ tall free). Persons in wheelchairs and blind persons free. Group discounts available. Checks accepted.
Special events	Gold Spike Day (mid-June)
Nearby attractions	Mount Rushmore, Black Hills, Badlands
Address	P. O. Box 1880, Hill City, SD 57745
Phone	(605) 574-2222

BLACK HILLS CENTRAL RAILROAD

The Black Hills Central offers a 2-hour, 20-mile round trip on its 1880 Train between Hill City and Keystone Junction, South Dakota, over a former Burlington line. More than half the route is on a 4 percent grade; the scenery includes mountain forests and meadows. Hill City is 27 miles from Rapid City in the Black Hills National Forest. Food and lodging are available in Hill City; motel reservations are advised in late July and early August. Reservations are recommended for the train ride — as is preparation for changeable weather.

Displays	24 coaches converted to sleeping rooms, HO gauge model railroad	
Dates open	Year-round, daily	
Admission	Model railroad: adults $1, children 50 cents	
Fares	Trolley: 50 cents	

Nearby attractions	Lookout Mountain, Rock City, Ruby Falls, Chickamauga Battlefield, Tennessee Valley Railroad Museum
Address	1400 Market Street, Chattanooga, TN 37402
Phone	(615) 266-5000

CHATTANOOGA CHOO-CHOO

Chattanooga's Terminal Station was opened in 1909 and closed in 1970. It reopened in 1973 not as a station but as a hotel, the Hilton Choo-Choo, with guest rooms in remodeled cars on tracks along the platforms and a dining room under the dome in what was the lobby. The hotel and restaurant complex includes a railroad-theme gift shop and a large operating model railroad. Outside a pair of street-cars shuttles guests between the parking lot and the hotel. To reach the Chattanooga Choo-Choo from I-24 in downtown Chattanooga, westbound take the Market Street exit and follow Market north to 14th. Eastbound on I-24, take the Lookout Mountain-Broad Street exit, 25th Street east to Market, and Market north to 14th.

Locomotives	3 steam, 3 diesel
Cars	Coaches
Displays	2 station buildings; mail, dining, sleeping, and business cars; artifacts
Dates open	Last weekend of March to first weekend of December, Saturdays and Sundays; June 15-Labor Day, daily. Open for groups of 40 or more at other times by appointment.
Schedule	Trains leave East Chattanooga hourly from 10:40 a.m. to 4:40 p.m. except

	Sundays, 12:40-4:40 Sundays; leave Grand Junction hourly 11:05-5:05 except Sundays; 1:05-5:05 Sundays. Charter trips available.
Fares	Adults $6, children 6-12 $3.50 (under 6 free). Checks and credit cards accepted. Group discounts available (reservations required).
Memberships	$35 annually
Special events	Mainline excursions, Arts and Craft Show, Grand Junction Festival — write

	for complete list.
Nearby attractions	Lookout Mountain, Rock City, Ruby Falls, Chickamauga Battlefield, Chattanooga Choo-Choo
Address	4119 Cromwell Road, Chattanooga, TN 37421
Phone	(615) 894-8028

TENNESSEE VALLEY RAILROAD MUSEUM

The Tennessee Valley Railroad Museum has two display sites connected by 3 miles of track. Trains shuttle between Grand Junction at 4119 Cromwell Road and East Chattanooga at 2200 North Chamberlain Avenue; the ride takes 14 minutes each way. Parking is available at both locations. To reach Grand Junction, take the Route 153-Chickamauga Dam exit from I-75, then the fourth exit, Jersey Pike, from 153. Turn left (south) on Jersey, then right almost immediately onto Cromwell Road. To reach East Chattanooga station from downtown, follow Broad Street north, Riverside Drive east, and Wilcox Boulevard east. At the fourth traffic light on Wilcox turn north on Chamberlain and go approximately half a mile to the depot. The Tennessee Valley Railroad Museum also sponsors mainline excursion trains — write for information on these trips.

Displays	Steam locomotive, flat car, caboose
Dates open	May-October, Thursday, Friday, and Saturday 10 a.m.-4 p.m., Sunday 1-4
Admission	Free, donations welcome
Memberships	Write for information.
Nearby attractions	Falls Mill, Hundred Oaks Castle, Old Jail Museum
Address	P. O. Box 53, Cowan, TN 37318
Phone	(615) 967-7365 for recorded information

COWAN RAILROAD MUSEUM

The CSX line from Nashville to Chattanooga (once Nashville, Chattanooga & St. Louis, later Louisville & Nashville) climbs over Cumberland Mountain south of Cowan, Tennessee. The grades are steep enough to require helpers in each direction; they are added to southbound trains at Cowan. The former station is now a museum housing a re-creation of a turn-of-the-century telegraph operator's office, various artifacts, and an HO scale model of the Cowan Pusher District. Cowan is on U. S. 41A and 64 12 miles west of Exit 135 of I-24 and about 15 miles north of the Alabama border. Food is available in Cowan; lodging can be found in Winchester, 7 miles west.

Displays	Steam locomotive, mail car, dining car, artifacts
Dates open	Summer, daily 9 a.m.-6 p.m.; winter, daily 10-4
Admission	Adults $3, children under 13 $1.75, senior citizens $2.25. Checks and credit cards accepted. Group discounts available.
Nearby attractions	Carl Perkins Music Museum
Address	Casey Jones Village, Jackson, TN 38305
Phone	(901) 668-1222

CASEY JONES HOME AND RAILROAD MUSEUM

On April 30, 1900, an Illinois Central passenger train ran into the rear of a freight at Vaughan, Mississippi. At the throttle was John Luther Jones, originally from Cayce, Kentucky. He was killed in the wreck. An engine-wiper named Wallace Saunders wrote a song about the incident, and a legend was born. The house Jones was living in has been moved to a park in Jackson, Tennessee, and has become a museum containing memorabilia and artifacts. The museum is located at Exit 80A (U. S. 45 bypass) of I-40 on the northwest side of Jackson. Casey Jones Village includes a restaurant; lodging is available nearby.

Displays	Union Pacific Big Boy No. 4018 and DDA40X 6913, GG1 4906, Santa Fe motor car M.160, several other steam locomotives, passenger and freight cars
Dates open	Thursdays and Fridays 9 a.m.-1 p.m., . Saturdays and Sunday 11-5
Admission	Adults $2, children under 17 $1. Checks accepted. Group discounts available.
Memberships	Write for information.
Special events	State Fair (October)
Nearby attractions	Fine Arts Museum, Natural History Museum, Aquarium, Cotton Bowl
Address	5716 Hillcroft Street, Dallas, TX 75227
Phone	(214) 421-8754

M. D. Monaghan

AGE OF STEAM RAILROAD MUSEUM

The Southwest Railroad Historical Society maintains a large collection of rolling stock at a site on Washington Street next to the Texas State Fair Park. The collection includes a complete passenger train of the 1920s and several steam locomotives. State Fair Park is just off the U. S. 67-80-I-30 freeway about 3 miles east of downtown Dallas.

Dallas

THE RAILROAD MUSEUM

Locomotives	1 steam, 1 diesel, 1 RDC
Cars	Coaches
Displays	More than three dozen passenger and freight cars and locomotives
Dates open	Daily 10 a.m.-5 p.m.
Schedule	Trains operate one weekend a month, on the average, on a holiday weekend if there is one. Trains leave at 1 and 3 p.m.
Admission	Adults $4, children 4-12 $2 (under 4 free), age 65 and over $3. Checks and credit cards accepted. Discounts available for groups of 15 or more.
Fares	$1 per person
Memberships	Write for information.
Special events	Annual model train exhibit, visiting locomotives and cars
Nearby attractions	The Strand Historic District, historic ships
Address	123 Rosenberg Avenue, Galveston, TX 77550
Phone	(409) 765-5700

RAILROAD MUSEUM AT THE CENTER FOR TRANSPORTATION & COMMERCE

The former Santa Fe station in Galveston, Texas, is now The Center for Transportation and Commerce. The museum displays include a large collection of cars and locomotives, an HO gauge model railroad, an orientation theater, and in The People's Gallery an exhibit titled "A Moment Frozen in Time": a waiting room populated with 39 life-size figures and equipped with a sound system for the conversations these people might have been having. One weekend a month on the average the museum offers steam-powered train rides over a mile of track on the Port of Galveston Wharves main line. The museum is at The Strand and 25th Street in Galveston. Food and lodging are available nearby.

Locomotives	2 steam	**Special events**	Jefferson Pilgrimage (first week of May),
Cars	Open cars, air-conditioned cars		Founders Day (July 4), Candle Light
Schedule	Daily from April 1, trains operate hourly		Tour (first week of December)
	10 a.m.-6 p.m. Charter trips operated.	**Nearby attractions**	Lake o' the Pines, Caddo Lake
Fares	Adults $5, children under 7 $4, age 65	**Address**	P. O. Drawer A, Jefferson, TX 75657
	and over $4.50. Checks accepted.		
	Group discounts available.		

JEFFERSON & CYPRESS BAYOU RAILROAD

Jefferson, 60 miles west of Shreveport, Louisiana, was once the largest inland port and the fifth largest city in Texas. Efforts to improve navigation in 1873 went awry and lowered the water level in Cypress Bayou so that navigation was no longer possible; by then railroads were replacing river boats. Jefferson has become a historic town with restored homes, antique shops, restaurants, and bed-and-breakfasts. The Jefferson & Cypress Bayou, scheduled to begin operation in April 1987, is a 3-foot-gauge steam-powered railroad that will offer a 5-mile, 45-minute ride along Big Cypress Bayou past the sites of lumber mills and iron works. Jefferson is in the northeast corner of Texas on U. S. 59, 15 miles north of Marshall and 55 miles south of Texarkana.

Locomotives	3 steam		trips available.	**Address**	P. O. Box 39, Rusk, TX 75785
Cars	Coaches	**Fares**	Adults $8 round trip, $6 one way; chil-	**Phone**	(214) 683-2561; in Texas, (800) 442-
Schedule	March 21, 1987-May 24, weekends;		dren 3-12 $6 round trip $4 one way.		8951
	May 25-August 16, Thursday-Monday;		Checks accepted.		
	August 22-November 1, weekends plus	**Nearby attractions**	Jim Hogg State Park, Caddoans Mounds		
	Labor Day: trains leave Rusk and Pales-		State Park, Tyler Rose Gardens, Tyler		
	tine 11 a.m., return at 3 p.m. Charter		State Park, Mission Tejas State Park		

TEXAS STATE RAILROAD HISTORICAL PARK

Construction of the Texas State Railroad was begun in 1896 to furnish transportation to an iron furnace that was part of a state prison at North Rusk, Texas. The iron plant closed in 1913 and the railroad was leased to the Texas & New Orleans (Southern Pacific) in 1921. For a period in the 1960s the line was leased to the Texas South-Eastern; then in 1972 the property was transferred to the Texas Parks & Wildlife Department to form a state historical park. The railroad offers a ride over 25 miles of track through rolling hills and pine woods. A one-way ride takes 90 minutes, and there is a 1-hour layover before the return trip — total, 4 hours. Reservations are recommended and can be booked well in advance; a tour of the locomotive cab is available during the hour before departure. The coaches are neither heated nor air-conditioned, so dress appropriately for the weather. Sandwiches, snacks, and ice cream are available on board; restaurants and lodging can be found in Rusk and Palestine. Rusk is on U. S. 69 and 84; Palestine is on U. S. 79, 84, and 287. They are north of Houston, southeast of Dallas, and southwest of Shreveport, Louisiana.

Cars	1 streetcar
Schedule	Tuesday-Friday, 11 a.m. and 2:30 p.m.; weekends, 10, 11, 1, 2, 3, and 4. Closed New Year's Day, Battle of Flowers Day, July 4, Labor Day, Thanksgiving, and Christmas.
Admission	To museums: adults $3, children 6-12 $1 (under 6 free), senior citizen, military, students with ID $1.50. Free Thursdays 3-9 p.m. Group discounts available.
Fares	Free with a current admission ticket to the Museum of Art, the Museum of Science/Technology/Transportation (at HemisFair Plaza; large collection of automobiles), or the Witte Museum (3801 Broadway — Texas history, natural science, and archeology)
Memberships	San Antonio Museum Association: individual $25, family $50
Nearby attractions	Museums, The Alamo, Texas Transportation Museum
Address	P. O. Box 2601, San Antonio, TX 78299-2601
Phone	(512) 226-5544; for recorded information, 225-3278

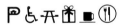

SAN ANTONIO MUSEUM ASSOCIATION

The San Antonio Museum Association operates "Old 300," the last remaining San Antonio streetcar (streetcars were replaced by buses in 1933) on a mile of track belong to the Pearl Brewery's Texas Transportation Co. in San Antonio. The ride begins at the Museum of Art, which is in the former Lone Star Brewery on 200 West Jones Avenue west of the San Antonio River. The streetcar stops at the Pearl Brewery, travels east along Jones to Austin Street, then returns to the art museum.

Locomotives	1 steam, 1 diesel
Cars	Cabooses
Displays	Steam locomotive, open trolley car, Pullman, Santa Fe business car, automobiles and trucks
Dates open	Weekends 9 a.m.-4 p.m., weather permitting
Schedule	Steam locomotive operates second Sunday of the month; diesel, every Sunday afternoon
Fares	Suggested donation, adults $2, children $1
Memberships	Write for information
Nearby attractions	San Antonio Museum Association trolley, The Alamo
Address	Longhorn Station 11731 Wetmore Road, San Antonio, TX 78427
Phone	(512) 490-3554

TEXAS TRANSPORTATION MUSEUM

The Texas Transportation Museum maintains an operating museum with .4 mile of track on Wetmore Road near the San Antonio airport. Operations are carried on with a Baldwin-built 0-4-0T and a General Electric 45-ton diesel; passengers ride in cabooses. Operation is subject to weather conditions. The displays include an open trolley car from Veracruz, Mexico; a 12 section-1 drawing room Pullman sleeping car; and a collection of vintage automobiles and trucks. Restaurants and lodging can be found nearby.

Locomotives	2 steam
Cars	Coaches, open cars, dining car
Displays	7 steam locomotives, 2 diesels, 1880 western village, working blacksmith shop
Schedule	Early May-Memorial Day, weekends at 10 a.m. and 2:30 p.m.; Memorial Day-Columbus Day, daily at 10 and 2:30; November 28-December 20, weekends at 11:45; December 21-24 and 26-31, daily at 11:45. Charter trips available.
Fares	Adults $9.50, children 3-12 $5, senior citizens $9. Credit cards and checks accepted (check guarantee card necessary). Discounts available for groups of 25 or more.
Special events	Flag Day (June 14) and Columbus Day — turn-of-the-century or Old West costume good for half-price ride
Nearby attractions	Wasatch Mountain State Park, Deer Creek and Strawberry Reservoirs
Address	600 West 100 South, Heber City, UT 84032
Phone	Heber, (801) 654-2900; Salt Lake City, (801) 531-6022

William J. Husa Jr.

HEBER CREEPER

The Utah Eastern Railroad opened its line from Heber City to Provo, Utah, in 1899. A year later it was acquired by the Rio Grande Western, which in turn became part of the Denver & Rio Grande Western. About 1970 the D&RGW abandoned the branch and it became a tourist railroad, the Wasatch Mountain Railway, nicknamed the Heber Creeper. The line offers a 3½-hour round trip covering 16 miles of track from Heber City to Vivian Park. The scenery along the route includes meadows, mountains, streams, and canyons. Food is available on the train and in Heber City, 46 miles southeast of Salt Lake City and 28 miles northeast of Provo on U. S. 40 and 189. Staff is on the premises year round.

Displays	2 operating steam locomotives, films, slide shows, 30 miles of roadbed
Dates open	Early June-Labor Day, daily 9:30 a.m.-5:30 p.m.; rest of the year 8-4:30. Closed some federal holidays during cool weather months. Steam locomotives on display 9-4 in May and September, 10:30-5:50 June-Labor Day.
Admission	Free (possible $2 per car charge, not confirmed at press time)
Special events	Anniversary Celebration (May 10), Railroaders' Festival (second Saturday in August)
Nearby attractions	Bear River Migratory Bird Refuge, Great Salt Lake
Address	P. O. Box W, Brigham City, UT 84032
Phone	(801) 471-2209

GOLDEN SPIKE NATIONAL HISTORIC SITE

As the Union Pacific and the Central Pacific built toward each other in 1869, they chose Promontory Summit, Utah, north of the Great Salt Lake, as their meeting point. The rails were joined on May 10, 1869, with a symbolic golden spike — it was the first North American rail line to connect the Atlantic and Pacific. In 1903 the Southern Pacific, which had absorbed the Central Pacific, began constructing a cutoff directly across the Great Salt Lake. It opened in 1904 and relegated the original route through Promontory to secondary status. The line was abandoned in 1942, and in recent years the monument marking the site of the Golden Spike ceremony has been augmented by a visitor center and colorful working replicas of the two locomotives that participated: Central Pacific *Jupiter* and Union Pacific No. 119. The 2700-acre site is operated by the National Park Service, U. S. Department of the Interior; park ranger talks are offered in summer. The Golden Spike National Historic Site is 32 miles west of Brigham City, Utah — follow Route 83 west to Promontory Junction, turn left and go 2 miles to the next junction, then right and another 5 miles. Food is not available there. Motels and restaurants can be found in Brigham City and Tremonton.

Bob Hayden

Locomotives	1 diesel
Cars	Flat cars with sides and benches
Displays	1 saddle-tank steam locomotive
Dates open	June through mid-October, Monday-Friday, 9:30 a.m.-3:30 p.m.
Fares	Adults $1.95; children 5-12, 50 cents. Checks and credit cards accepted. Group rate, $1.50 per person.
Nearby attractions	State Capitol, Morse Sugar House, Cabot Creamery
Address	Box 482, Barre, VT 05641
Phone	(802) 476-3115

P & ⅌ 🎁 ■

ROCK OF AGES CORPORATION

The Rock of Ages Corporation in Barre, Vermont, offers guided tours of its granite quarrying and manufacturing operations — the world's largest — and a ¾-mile, 25-minute train ride between two quarries. On display is one of the saddletank steam locomotives that was replaced by diesels in 1958. To reach the quarry, take Route 63 east from Exit 6 of I-89 through South Barre to the Tourist Center at Graniteville. From the center of Barre, take South Main Street and follow the signs. Barre is approximately halfway between Boston and Montreal. Food and lodging are available in Barre.

Locomotives	5 diesels
Cars	Steel coaches, ex-Rutland wooden coach and combine
Schedule	June 20-September 7, 1987, daily; September 12-20, weekends; September 26-October 12, daily; October 17-October 25, weekends: leave Bellows Falls 11 a.m. and 1:30 p.m., leave Chester 12:05 p.m. Charter trips available beginning May 16.
Fares	Adults $7, children 5-12 $5, age 55 and over $6.30. Checks accepted. Discounts available for groups of 20 or more.
Special events	Railfan Weekend (June 13-14, 1987), F. Nelson Blount Memorial Trip to Summit (September 6, 1987)
Nearby attractions	Santa's Land, Fort No. 4, Green Mountains
Address	P. O. Box 498, Bellows Falls, VT 05101-0498
Phone	(802) 463-3069

GREEN MOUNTAIN RAILROAD

After the Rutland Railway ceased operation in 1961, freight service on the line between Bellows Falls and Rutland was restored by the Green Mountain Railroad, and Steamtown USA began operating excursion trains between Bellows Falls and Chester, 13 miles. Steamtown moved to Scranton, Pennsylvania, in 1984, and excursion service was operated for part of that season by Vermont Historical Railroad Train in cooperation with the Green Mountain.

In 1985 Green Mountain began operating the excursion trains itself. The equipment for the trains includes two former Rutland cars, a combination baggage-coach and a coach; Green Mountain's locomotive roster includes the last former Rutland locomotive still in New

England, RS1 No. 405. The train leaves the Bellows Falls station (also used by Amtrak's *Montrealer*) and follows the west bank of the Connecticut River for 2 miles, then follows the Williams River to Chester. The ride takes 1 hour and 40 minutes. A round trip originating in Chester is also possible.

From I-91 take Exit 5 or Exit 6, then U. S. 5 to downtown Bellows Falls. Take Canal Street to Depot Street or Bridge Street to Island Street. Vermont's signage law forbids all but the most modest signs, so it's helpful to know the station in Bellows Falls is on an island formed by the Connecticut River and a power canal. Food and lodging are available in Bellows Falls.

Locomotives	6 diesel
Cars	Coaches
Displays	Snowplow, caboose
Schedule	Picnic train: late June through August, leave Morrisville Tuesdays, Thursdays, and Saturdays 10 a.m., return at 2:45. Fall Foliage Train, mid-September through mid-October, leave Morrisville Tuesdays, Thursdays, Saturdays, and Sundays at 10 and 2 for 2¾-hour trip. Charter trips available.
Fares	Picnic train: adults $15, children 5-13 $10; Fall Foliage Excursions: Adults $12, children 5-13 $8. Checks and credit cards accepted. Discounts for groups of 25 or more.
Nearby attractions	Stowe, Mt. Mansfield, St. J. & L.C. Railroad
Address	Stafford Avenue, Morrisville, VT 05661
Phone	(802) 888-4255

LAMOILLE VALLEY RAILROAD

The Lamoille Valley operates freight service over a portion of the former St. Johnsbury & Lake Champlain and offers excursions from Morrisville, Vermont. The line includes one of the last railroad covered bridges in the U. S. Picnic Excursions run to Joe's Pond, 35 miles, with enough time for lunch there. Inexpensive box lunches can be purchased before departure, or you may bring your own. Fall Foliage Excursions go as far as Walden, 30 miles, second highest railroad pass in New England. Snacks are available on the train. Reservations are advised. Access for the handicapped is limited; inquire when you make reservations. Restaurants and lodging can be found in Morrisville; Stowe, a major resort town, is 10 miles to the south. Morrisville is north of Montpelier and about halfway between Burlington and St. Johnsbury on Routes 12, 15, and 100.

Locomotives	Diesel	**Memberships**	Write for information.
Cars	Coaches, snack car, lounge car	**Nearby attractions**	Maple Grove Maple Museum, Fairbanks
Displays	A museum is being developed in the station at Danville, 7 miles west of St. Johnsbury		Science Museum, St. Johnsbury Atheneum and Art Gallery, Lamoille Valley Railroad
Schedule	September 19, 20, 26, and 27, October 3, 4, 10, and 11, leave St. Johnsbury 9 a.m. and 1 p.m.	**Address**	P. O. Box 636, St. Johnsbury, VT 05819
Fares	Adults $15, children under 17 $5. Checks accepted. Group discounts available.	**Phone**	(802) 748-3685; St. Johnsbury Chamber of Commerce 748-3678

St. J. & L. C. RAILROAD

Excursions during the fall foliage season are offered over the east end of the Lamoille Valley Railroad by the St. J. & L. C. Railroad in cooperation with the St. Johnsbury Chamber of Commerce. Trains leave St. Johnsbury at 9 a.m. and 1 p.m. on weekends for a 3-hour round trip to Greensboro Bend, 28½ miles west. Reservations are advised. Snacks are available on the train, and a chicken barbecue lunch is available in St. Johnsbury from 11 to 1. Food and lodging can be found in St. Johnsbury, in the northeast part of the state at the intersection of I-93 and I-91. From Exit 21 of I-91 head down toward the town. Go straight at the traffic light at the intersection of U. S. 2, then take the next right and follow signs to the station, which is down near the Sleepers River — south of U. S. 2, west of U. S. 5, and east of I-91.

Displays	Central Vermont 4-6-0, private car *Grand Isle*, station, memorabilia		counts available (reservations required).
		Memberships	Write for information.
Dates open	Mid-May through mid-October, 9 a.m.-5 p.m.	**Nearby attractions**	Lake Champlain
		Address	Shelburne, Vermont 05482
Admission	Adults $9, children 6-17 $3.50 (under 6 free). Credit cards accepted. Group dis-	**Phone**	(802) 985-3346; 985-3344 for recorded information

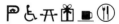

SHELBURNE MUSEUM

The Shelburne Museum grew from the Americana collection of Electra Havemeyer Webb, wife of a descendant of Cornelius Vanderbilt. After World War Two the collection became a museum, and the 45-acre site has grown to resemble a good-size village. The village includes a railroad station — the Shelburne Station of the Rutland Railway — with a short train on the track in front. Nearby is Delaware & Hudson's Lake Champlain steamer *Ticonderoga*. Food is available at the museum, and restaurants and lodging can be found in Shelburne and in Burlington, 7 miles north.

St. Johnsbury   Shelburne   VERMONT-157

Displays	50 locomotives and cars, including Virginian rectifier electric and 0-8-0 steam switcher, Pennsylvania GG1, Wabash E8 No. 1009, Electro-Motive's 10,000th diesel unit
Dates open	Monday-Saturday 10 a.m.-5 p.m., Sunday 12-5
Admission	Adults $2, children 3-12 $1 (under 3 free), age 60 and over $1.60. Checks and credit cards accepted. Group discount available.
Memberships	Write for information.
Nearby attractions	Fine Arts Museum, outdoor market, Science Museum
Address	303 Norfolk Avenue, Roanoke, VA 24011
Phone	(703) 342-5670

VIRGINIA MUSEUM OF TRANSPORTATION

The Roanoke Transportation Museum was owned and operated by the city of Roanoke from 1963 to 1976. It came under the direction of a nonprofit corporation in 1977. In 1983 it was designated as the official transportation museum of the commonwealth of Virginia, and in 1985 it received its present name. Its collection includes two Norfolk & Western locomotives, 4-8-4 No. 611 and 2-6-6-4 No. 1218, that are in active excursion service. The museum is three blocks west of the city market in downtown Roanoke. To get there, leave I-581 at Exit 6, Elm Avenue. Go west on Elm, north (right) on Jefferson, west (left) on Salem, and north (right) on Third to the museum. Food and lodging are available in Roanoke.

Locomotives	1 steam
Cars	1 open car, 1 parlor-observation car, 1 baggage-parlor car
Displays	Railroad artifacts in station
Schedule	June 7-September 7, weekends and holidays, noon-4:30 p.m.
Fares	50 cents (babies free)
Special events	Taste of Skagit Tulip Festival (April 2-5, 1987), Anacortes Arts & Crafts Festival (first weekend of August)
Nearby attractions	Ferry to San Juan Islands, Maritime Museum
Address	387 Campbell Lake Road, Anacortes, WA 98221
Phone	(206) 293-2634

ANACORTES RAILWAY

The Anacortes Railway is an 18″-gauge railroad in downtown Anacortes, Washington. It offers a .4-mile ride between the former Great Northern depot at 7th and R Avenue and the corner of 4th and R; the track is being extended to 5th and I. The line's steam locomotive was rebuilt in 1969 from a compressed-air mining locomotive built in 1909. Food and lodging are available within three blocks of the railroad. Anacortes is on an island west of Mount Vernon, Wash., about 70 miles north of Seattle.

Anacortes

MOUNT RAINIER SCENIC RAILROAD

Locomotives	3 steam, 2 diesel
Cars	Coaches, open car with benches
Displays	Steam locomotives, logging equipment
Schedule	May 23-September 20, weekends; June 15-Labor Day, daily: leave 11 a.m. and 1:15 and 3:30 p.m.
Fares	Adults $6.50, children 12-18 $4.50, children 4-11 $3.50 (under 4 free), age 60 and over $5.50, family (parents and children under 18) $17. Checks accepted. Discount of 15 percent for groups of 25 or more with reservation and deposit.
Special events	Railfan Days, trips over Chehalis Western and former Milwaukee Road
Nearby attractions	Mount Rainier, Mount St. Helens
Address	P. O. Box 921, Elbe, WA 98330
Phone	(206) 569-2588

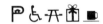

MOUNT RAINIER SCENIC RAILROAD

The Mount Rainier Scenic Railroad operates over a 7-mile portion of a former Milwaukee Road branch line (originally the Tacoma Eastern) from Elbe, Washington, to a logging display and picnic area at Mineral. The line includes an 800-foot-long trestle over the Nisqually River and short stretches of 3 percent grade and affords a view of Mount Rainier. Live music and entertainment are featured during the train ride. Train operation is subject to cancellation in bad weather. Elbe is about 40 miles south-southeast of Tacoma on Route 7; from the south, take U. S. 12 east from I-5 to Morton, then follow Route 7 north to Elbe. Snacks are available at Elbe and Mineral. The nearest restaurant is in Ashford, 6 miles east of Elbe; the nearest lodging is 3 miles northwest of Elbe.

Cars	3 streetcars
Schedule	Memorial Day-Labor Day, weekends and holidays 8:30 a.m.-11 p.m., Monday-Friday 7 a.m.-11 p.m.; rest of the year, weekends and holidays 10:30-5:30, Monday-Friday 7-6. Cars run every 20 minutes from mid-morning to early evening and every 30 minutes at other times, except for early evening, when headways are 40-50 minutes.
Fares	Age 6-64, 60 cents (under 6 free); age 65 and over, 15 cents; or valid Metro pass or transfer
Special events	Free rides Memorial Day weekend
Nearby attractions	Underground Seattle, Pike Place Public Market, Seattle Aquarium, Waterfront Park, ferries, Seattle Center, Space Needle
Address	Metro, 821 Second Avenue, Seattle, WA 98104
Phone	(206) 447-4800

WATERFRONT STREETCAR

Seattle's transit system, Metro, includes a streetcar line along the waterfront between South Main Street and Broad Street. The streetcars on the line are from Melbourne, Australia, and were built in 1927. At each station there are ticket-vending and bill-changing machines. The south terminal of the line, Pioneer Square, is about four blocks west of the Amtrak station. The north terminal at Broad Street is six blocks southwest of the Seattle Center, site of the 1962 World's Fair.

Seattle

Locomotives	5 steam
Cars	Coaches, observation car, open car, occasionally a caboose
Displays	Steam, gasoline, diesel, and electric locomotives, interurbans, trolleys, passenger and freight cars, logging and mining railroad equipment
Schedule	April-October, Sundays; also Saturdays and holidays Memorial Day weekend through September: leave Snoqualmie 11 a.m. and 12:30, 2, and 3:30, also 5 p.m. Memorial Day-Labor Day; leave North Bend 30 minutes later. Charter trips available.
Fares	Adults $5, children 5-15 $3 (under 5 free), age 62 and over $4. Discount of 20 percent available for groups of 20 or more making a single ticket purchase.
Memberships	Write for information.
Special events	School Train (May), Railfan Special (June), Autumn Harvest and Wine Tasting (September), Spook Train (last weekend of October), Santa Train (two weekends in December)
Nearby attractions	Snoqualmie Falls, state fish hatchery, hiking trails
Address	P. O. Box 459, Snoqualmie, WA 98065
Phone	(206) 888-3030; 746-4025 year-round and for recorded information

Kenneth G. Johnsen

PUGET SOUND & SNOQUALMIE VALLEY RAILROAD

The Puget Sound Railway Historical Association operates 5 miles of a former Northern Pacific branch between North Bend and Snoqualmie, Washington, as the Puget Sound & Snoqualmie Valley Railroad. The train takes 70 minutes to make the 10-mile round trip along a scenic valley; on the way it passes a 268-foot-high waterfall. On display are more than 100 locomotives and cars. Passengers may board at either North Bend or Snoqualmie; both are just off I-90 about 30 miles east of Seattle. Food and drink are not allowed on the train, but there is a snack bar next to the Snoqualmie depot and there are restaurants in Snoqualmie and North Bend. Lodging can be found in North Bend; reservations are advised in summer.

Locomotives	2 steam, 1 diesel, 1 locomotive crane
Cars	Covered flat cars with benches, caboose
Displays	Logging and logging railroad equipment
Schedule	Memorial Day-Labor Day, weekends and holidays, half-hourly from 11 a.m. to 6 p.m. Charter trips available.
Fares	Adults $1.50; children 3-11, 75 cents; age 65 and over, 75 cents. Local checks accepted. Group discounts available by prior arrangement.
Memberships	Tacoma Chapter, NRHS — write for information
Special events	Steam Logging Spectacular (April, biennial), School Days (May 28-29), Speeder Festival (September 12), Santa Train (December 5, 6, 12, and 13)
Nearby attractions	Fort Defiance, Old Steilacoom, Mount Rainier, Mount St. Helens, Seattle
Address	Tacoma Chapter, NRHS, P. O. Box 340, Tacoma, WA 98401
Phone	(206) 752-0047

P &. 开

CAMP SIX LOGGING EXHIBIT

The Tacoma Chapter of the National Railway Historical Society operates the Point Defiance, Quinault & Klickitat Railroad on the property of the Camp Six Logging Exhibit of the Western Forest Industries Museum. The museum is in Point Defiance Park in the city of Tacoma, at the tip of the peninsula that separates Commencement Bay from The Narrows. Food is available within the park, and there are restaurants in Ruston, 5 minutes away.

Tacoma

Locomotives	1 steam, 1 diesel, 1 gasoline
Cars	Coaches, parlor-observation
Schedule	First Saturday of June through first Saturday of September, Saturdays and Tuesdays only, leave Wickersham noon and 2 p.m. Charter trips and charter cars operated.
Fares	Adults $6, children under 18 $3. Checks accepted. Group discounts available.
Special events	Valentine Train, Easter Train, Santa Claus Christmas Trains (December Saturdays before Christmas) — reservations required
Nearby attractions	Puget Sound, North Cascades National Park, Mt. Baker National Forest
Address	P. O. Box 91, Acme, WA 98220
Phone	(206) 595-2218

LAKE WHATCOM RAILWAY

The Lake Whatcom Railway operates over a 4-mile portion of the former Northern Pacific branch from Wickersham to Bellingham, Washington. The usual motive power is Northern Pacific 0-6-0 No. 1070; the coaches are also former Northern Pacific equipment. Wickersham is on State Route 9 southeast of Bellingham and about 30 miles south of the Canadian border. Take the Route 20 exit from I-5 and drive 7 miles east to Sedro Woolley, then 11 miles north to Wickersham. Refreshments are available on the train. There are restaurants in Acme, 5 miles north of Wickersham, and motels in Sedro Woolley.

Cars	2 streetcars
Schedule	Mid-April through October, Saturdays hourly 10 a.m.-4 p.m., Sundays hourly noon-5; July and early August, Monday-Friday at 6, 7, and 8 p.m.; also Memorial Day, July 4, and Labor Day. Charters available.
Fares	Adults $3, children 6-12 $1.50 (under 6 free if they do not occupy a seat), age 60 and over $1.50. Charters, $150 for 2 hours boarding at carbarn, $175 boarding elsewhere. Checks accepted.
Memberships	Write for information
Nearby attractions	Yakima Museum, Heritage Cultural Center
Address	Yakima Interurban Lines Association, P. O. Box 124, Yakima, WA 98907
Phone	(509) 575-1700

Kenneth G. Johnsen

YAKIMA INTERURBAN TROLLEY

In 1974 as a bicentennial project the Yakima Valley Transportation Company, an electrically operated Union Pacific subsidiary, acquired two 1906-vintage streetcars from Oporto, Portugal, and placed them in excursion service. Of necessity the streetcar operation must mesh with YVT's freight schedules. Trips open to the public cover about 1½ miles of track on weekend mornings and summer weekday evenings. Morning trips depart from Whitney School at 44th Avenue and West Nob Hill Boulevard and go to Harwood (Saturday) or Ahtanum (Sunday); summer evening trips depart from the Selah Civic Center on South First in Selah. Charter trips can be arranged to cover any of YVT's track from the carbarn at 507 South 5th Avenue in Yakima. Food and lodging can be found in Yakima, Selah, and Wapato. Yakima is on I-82 about 145 miles southeast of Seattle.

Yakima

Locomotives	6 steam, 1 diesel
Cars	Open excursion cars
Displays	Logging equipment, passenger cars, cabooses, steam and diesel locomotives
Schedule	To Bald Knob (4½ hours): Memorial Day-Labor Day, daily except Mondays; Labor Day through October, weekends; first two weeks of October, Wednesday-Sunday; leave Cass at noon. To Whittaker (2 hours): Saturday before Memorial Day-Labor Day, daily; Labor Day through October, weekends; leave Cass 11 a.m., 1 p.m., 3 p.m. (11 a.m. runs begin mid-June); first two weeks of October, Wednesday-Friday, leave Cass 1 and 3; weekends leave Cass 11, 1, and 3. Charter trips available.
Fares	Adults $9.50 to Bald Knob, $7 to Whittaker; children 6-11 $4 to Bald Knob, $3 to Whittaker (under 6 free); $1 discount for West Virginia seniors. Checks accepted. Group discounts available.
Special events	Railfan Weekend (May), Saturday night dinner trains (June-August)
Nearby attractions	National Radio Astronomy Observatory, Seneca Caverns, Smoke Hole Caverns, Monongahela National Forest, Pearl Buck birthplace
Address	P. O. Box 107, Cass, WV 24927
Phone	(304) 456-4300

CASS SCENIC RAILROAD

The Cass Scenic Railroad was established in 1961 by the state of West Virginia to operate excursion trains over a former logging railroad out of the town of Cass. It has become one of the most successful and interesting tourist railroads in North America. The line to the summit of Bald Knob climbs 2390 feet in 11 miles and includes stretches of 10 percent grade — up 10 feet for every 100 feet forward.

Passengers may also choose a ride to Whittaker, 4 miles from Cass. Food and lodging are available in Cass; former lumber company houses have been refurbished for use as vacation lodging (reservations are necessary and can be made through the railroad). Cass is near the Virginia border about halfway between Covington, Va., and Elkins, W. Va.

Cars	3 interurbans, 1 rapid transit car, 1 streetcar
Displays	Artifacts, cars under restoration
Dates open	Memorial Day weekend through October, weekends (closed holidays) 11 a.m.-5 p.m.; mid-June through August, also open Wednesdays, Thursdays, and Fridays 11-3
Schedule	Leave East Troy 11:30, 1, and 2:30, also 4 p.m. on weekends. Charter trips available.
Fares	Adults $4, children 6-12 $2. Checks accepted. Group discounts available.
Memberships	Write for information.
Nearby attractions	Lake Geneva, Old World Wisconsin, Kettle Moraine State Forest, Kettle Moraine Railway
Address	Box 436, East Troy, WI 53120
Phone	(414) 642-3263 during operations; year round 542-5573

EAST TROY ELECTRIC RAILROAD

In 1939 the Milwaukee Electric Railway & Light Company abandoned its interurban line to East Troy, Wisconsin. The village of East Troy purchased the outermost 6 miles of the line to connect the industries in the village with the Soo Line. The line was operated electrically until fairly recent times. In 1984 the village offered the Wisconsin Trolley Museum, then located at North Prairie, operating rights on the railroad. The museum moved to East Troy the following year. Cars operate on 5 miles of track between East Troy and the intersection of County Highways ES and J near Mukwonago. The round trip takes 50 minutes. East Troy is about 35 miles southwest of Milwaukee on Route 15. To reach the museum, take Exit 42 (Route 20) from Route 15 and go west on 20 a short distance to County Highway ES. Turn left on ES and follow it into East Troy, then turn right on Church Street and go two blocks to the museum. There are restaurants in East Troy; lodging can be found in Lake Geneva about 15 miles south.

East Troy

Displays	Approximately 80 locomotives and cars
Dates open	May 1-October 1, daily, 9 a.m.-5 p.m.
Admission	Adults $4, children 6-12 $2.50, age 62 and over $3.50. Checks and credit cards accepted. Group discounts available.
Memberships	Write for information.
Nearby attractions	Green Bay Packer Hall of Fame, Heritage Hill State Park
Address	2285 South Broadway, Green Bay, WI 54304
Phone	(414) 435-7245

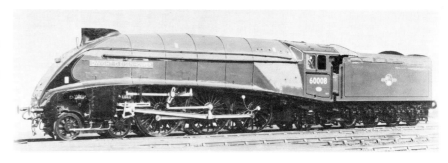

RAIL AMERICA — THE NATIONAL RAILROAD MUSEUM

Rail America has an extensive collection of locomotives and cars, including a number of large, modern steam locomotives, among them a Union Pacific Big Boy, a Santa Fe 2-10-4, and a Milwaukee Road 4-8-4. The museum also has such exotic items as a General Motors Aerotrain of 1955 (a lightweight streamliner with cars based on GM's intercity bus body and a locomotive styled along the lines of a 1955 Oldsmobile) and the London & North Eastern locomotive and cars that served as wartime staff headquarters for Dwight Eisenhower and Winston Churchill. Admission to the museum includes a train ride on a 1-mile loop of track; there is also a 12"-gauge live-steam train in operation. The museum is located on the bank of the Fox River on the south side of Green Bay. Food and lodging are available in Green Bay.

Displays	2500 railroad models, operating layouts	**Nearby attractions**	Mid-Continent Railway Museum, Circus World Museum, Wisconsin Dells
Dates open	Mid-May to mid-September, daily 10 a.m.-6 p.m.	**Address**	Route 1, Box 154B, Herwig Road, Reedsburg, WI 53959
Admission	Adults $3, children 6-12 $1.50 (under 6 free). Credit cards accepted. Group discounts available.	**Phone**	(608) 254-8050

PARK LANE MODEL RAILROAD MUSEUM

The Park Lane Model Railroad Museum has a large collection of railroad models of all scales and ages plus several operating layouts and layouts under construction. It is just a few minutes southwest of Exit 89 (Route 23) of I-90 and I-94 at Lake Delton, near Wisconsin Dells. From the interstate follow Route 23 west; the museum is at the intersection of 23 and Herwig Road. Food and lodging can be found in Lake Delton and Wisconsin Dells.

CAMP ⑤ FIVE

Locomotives	1 steam
Cars	Coaches, cabooses
Dates open	June 23-August 27 (closed Sundays)
Schedule	Trains leave Laona hourly from 11 a.m. to 2 p.m.; trains leave Camp 5 Farm at 11:20, 12:20, 1:20, 3, and 4. Charter trips available for groups of 200 or more.
Admission	Adults $7.50, children 3-12 $3.50, 2 adults and 2-4 children $20, tax additional. Checks accepted. Discounts available for groups of 30 or more (reservations required).
Nearby attractions	Nicolet National Forest
Address	Camp 5 Museum Foundation, Laona, WI 54541 (summer); 1011 Eighth Street, Wausau, WI 54401 (winter)
Phone	(715) 674-3620 (depot), 674-3414 (office), 845-5544 (winter)

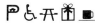

LAONA & NORTHERN RAILWAY

One of the attractions at Camp 5, a logging museum at Laona, Wisconsin, is the Laona & Northern's "Lumberjack Special" steam train ride to Camp 5 Farm. The train makes a 2½-mile, 15-minute run through forests and fields. The steam locomotive is a 2-6-2 built by Vulcan Iron Works, Wilkes-Barre, Pennsylvania, in 1916. Other attractions at Camp 5 include a logging museum, a forest tour, and a wild and domestic animal corral. Snacks are available at Camp 5. Restaurants and lodging can be found in Laona, Crandon (12 miles west), and Rhinelander (40 miles west). Laona is on U. S. 8 in northeast Wisconsin about 90 miles north-northwest of Green Bay.

Locomotives	5 steam, 1 diesel
Cars	Steel and wood coaches
Displays	Turn-of-the-century locomotives, freight and passenger cars, and work equipment
Dates open	May 12-September 7, daily 10:30 a.m.-5 p.m.; September 12-October 11, weekends 10:30-5
Schedule	Trains leave at 11, 1, 2:30, and 4. Charter trips available.
Fares	Adults $6, children 5-15 $3, age 62 and over $5. Checks and credit cards accepted. Group discounts available.
Memberships	Mid-Continent Railway Historical Society — write for information.
Special events	Autumn Color Weekends (first two weekends of October), Snow Train (third weekend of February)
Nearby attractions	Circus World Museum, Park Lane Model Railroad Museum, Wisconsin Dells, Devils Lake State Park
Address	P. O. Box 55, North Freedom, WI 53951
Phone	(608) 522-4261

MID-CONTINENT RAILWAY MUSEUM

The Mid-Continent Railway Museum was founded in 1959 and moved from its original location at Hillsboro, Wisconsin, to North Freedom in 1963. It operates 4 miles of a former Chicago & North Western branch line originally built to serve iron mines in the area. The museum specializes in equipment and operation of the 1885-1915 era and offers a 55-minute train ride through woods and farmland. North Freedom is about 45 miles northwest of Madison. The museum's Chicago & North Western 4-6-0 No. 1385 has been operated and exhibited system-wide by the C&NW in recent years.

To reach the museum from the south and east take the Route 33 exit from I-90 and I-94 west of Portage; follow 33 west to West Baraboo. From the north, leave the interstate on U. S. 12 south of Wisconsin Dells and go south to West Baraboo; from there follow Route 136 and County Highway PF to North Freedom. There are restaurants in North Freedom and motels in Baraboo.

Locomotives	2 steam, 1 gasoline, 1 gas-electric
Cars	Steel coaches and combine, cabooses, open car
Schedule	Sundays June through third Sunday of October plus Labor Day, 1, 2:30, and 4 p.m., also 11 a.m. during October. Charter trips available.
Fares	Adults $5, children 3-11 $2.50 (under 3 free), age 60 and over $4.50. Checks accepted. Group discounts available.
Nearby attractions	Kettle Moraine State Forest, East Troy Electric Railroad, Holy Hill, Mapleton Cheese Factory
Address	Box 247, North Lake, WI 53064
Phone	(414) 782-8074, 966-2866

Jerrold F. Hilton

KETTLE MORAINE RAILWAY

The Kettle Moraine Railway operates a 4½-mile portion of the former North Lake branch of the Milwaukee Road. The train ride through the rolling countryside includes several steep grades and takes approximately an hour. The usual locomotive is ex-McCloud River 2-6-2 No. 9. North Lake is on the northwest fringes of suburban Milwaukee. To reach the station at North Lake, take State Route 83 north from either I-94 or U. S. 16 about 23 miles west of downtown Milwaukee. North Lake is 9 miles north of I-94. There are restaurants in North Lake; motels can be found along I-94 in toward Milwaukee.

North Lake

Locomotives	3 steam (all 0-6-0)
Cars	Wood coaches, mountain observation car
Displays	Business, freight, and work cars
Dates open	May 16-September 7, daily 10 a.m.-6 p.m. (until 4 weekdays in May and June); September 8-October 12, weekends and holidays 10-5
Admission	Adults $4.50, youths 12-17 $3.25, children 3-11 $2 (under 3 free), age 65 and over $3.25. Checks and credit cards accepted. Group discounts available.
Fares	$1.50 per person for complete loop, but you may get off at any station and reboard later.
Memberships	Write for information.
Special events	None specifically railroad-oriented
Nearby attractions	Glenbow Museum, Calgary Tower, Calgary Zoo and Prehistoric Park, Calgary Stampede, Banff National Park
Address	1900 Heritage Drive S. W., Calgary, AB T2V 2X3
Phone	(403) 255-1182; for recorded information 252-1858

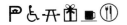

George Drury

HERITAGE PARK

Heritage Park presents a re-creation of life in western Canada before 1915. More than 100 antique buildings have been acquired and moved to the 66-acre park to portray a town; only a few structures are reproductions. Circling the park is a ⅞-mile loop of track; every 10 to 15 minutes a steam-powered train makes a circuit of the loop, stopping at three stations. Passengers may get off at any station to see the exhibits nearby, then reboard the train. A roundhouse and turntable are open to view. A streetcar carries visitors from the parking lot to the main gate. There are restaurants and snack bars in the park; food and lodging can be found in Calgary. The park is in southwest Calgary on the east shore of Glenmore Reservoir. Take Glenmore Trail (the South-West Bypass) to 14th Street S. W., then 14th Street south to Heritage Drive.

Cars	2 streetcars
Displays	Cars under restoration
Dates open	May 22-October 7, daily 10 a.m.-6 p.m.; September 12-October 5, weekends noon-6
Admission	Adults $4, youths 13-17 $2.50, children 6-12 $1.50, senior citizens $2, families $11. Group discounts available.
Fares	Free
Memberships	Write for information.
Nearby attractions	Fort Edmonton Park, Alberta Game Farm, Jasper National Park
Address	3543 106A Street, Edmonton, AB T6J 1A7
Phone	(403) 436-5565

EDMONTON RADIAL RAILWAY SOCIETY

The Edmonton Radial Railway Society was formed to build and operate a streetcar line in Fort Edmonton Park, which has areas representing 1905, 1920, and 1950 street scenes. The society has restored two Edmonton streetcars (the system was converted to buses in 1951) and is working on several others. The streetcars operate through the streets of the park. The 1.2-mile ride takes 15-20 minutes. Rides are included in the price of admission to the park. Streetcars can be chartered for group tours. The park is on the south bank of the North Saskatchewan River west of Whitemud Drive in southwest Edmonton. Food is available in the park, and lodging can be found in the city of Edmonton.

Edmonton

Displays	Complete *Trans-Canada Limited* train
Dates open	June-August, daily 9 a.m.-8 p.m.; rest of the year Sunday-Thursday noon-5 (to 8 Monday and Tuesday)
Admission	Free
Memberships	Write for information.
Special events	Great Train dinners
Nearby attractions	Fort Steele Historic Park
Address	Box 400, Cranbrook, BC V1C 4H9
Phone	(604) 489-3918

CRANBROOK RAILWAY MUSEUM

The Cranbrook Railway Museum, operated by the Cranbrook Archives, Museum, and Landmark Foundation, features a restored *Trans-Canada Limited* train, one of ten built in 1929 for the Canadian Pacific Railway. The train includes a baggage-sleeper that was used as a crew dormitory, a dining car, a sleeper, a solarium-lounge, and a business car. A steam locomotive will be added to the display in the future. The cars were displayed at the Via Rail pavilion at the 1986 World's Fair in Vancouver. The museum is at 1 Van Horne Street North. Cranbrook is in southeast British Columbia on Routes 3 and 95; food and lodging can be found in the town.

Locomotives	1 steam
Cars	5 wood coaches, 1 steel coach
Schedule	June-September, Sundays, leave Winnipeg 11:30 a.m. and 3 p.m. Charter trips available.
Fares	Adults $8, youths 12-17 $5, children 3-11 $4, age 65 and over $6
Memberships	Write for information.
Nearby attractions	Manitoba Museum of Man and Nature, Western Canada Aviation Museum, Winnipeg Mint
Address	Vintage Locomotive Society, Box 217, St. James P. O., Winnipeg, MB R3J 3R4
Phone	(204) 284-2690

William J. Husa Jr.

PRAIRIE DOG CENTRAL

Using the name Prairie Dog Central, the Vintage Locomotive Society operates excursion trains from Winnipeg northwest to Grosse Isle, Manitoba, over 18 miles of Canadian National Railway's Oakpoint Subdivision. The locomotive is an ex-Canadian Pacific 4-4-0, built in 1882 by Dübs & Company of Glasgow, Scotland. It is the oldest locomotive operating on a Class 1 railroad in Canada. The train departs from Canadian National's St. James station on Portage Avenue west of St. James Street, west of downtown Winnipeg and southeast of the airport. The 36-mile round trip takes 2 hours. Refreshments and souvenirs are available on the train; souvenirs can also be purchased at the station.

Winnipeg

Locomotives	1 steam, 1 diesel
Cars	Coaches, open cars, dining car
Displays	Snowplow, freight and passenger cars, work equipment
Schedule	Mid-May to mid-June and late September, weekends at 1:30 and 3 p.m.; late June-Labor Day, daily at 1:30 and 3, Thursday-Saturday also at 9:45 and 4:30, Sunday also at 4:30 and 6:30; week after Labor Day, daily at 1:30 and 3; October, weekends at 2:15 to Baltimore. Dinner train: June, weekends at 6:30; July-Labor Day, Monday, Wednesday, and weekends at 6:30; September, weekends at 5:45; October, Wednesday at 12:30 and weekends at 4. Charter trips available.
Fares	Salem: Adults $5, children 6-12 $2.50 (under 6 free), age 55 and over $4.25. Baltimore: $7/$3.50/$5.50. Credit cards accepted. Dinner train $17.95-$23.95 plus tax depending on menu. Group discounts available.
Memberships	Write for information.
Special events	Railfan Day (September)
Nearby attractions	Albert County Museum, William Henry Steeves House
Address	P. O. Box 70, Hillsborough, NB E0A 1X0
Phone	(506) 734-3195; in New Brunswick 800-332-3989

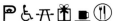

SALEM & HILLSBOROUGH RAILROAD

The New Brunswick Division of the Canadian Railroad Historical Association operates the Salem & Hillsborough Railroad over part of a Canadian National branch between Salisbury and Hillsborough, N. B. Most of the S&H's excursion trains run from Hillsborough to Salem, 5 miles, and return, but the dinner trains and the fall foliage excursions go to Baltimore, 11 miles from Hillsborough. Reservations are necessary for the dinner trains. Refreshments are available on the train, and food and lodging can be found in Hillsborough, about 20 miles south of Moncton. The Hillsborough station is on Main Street (Route 114).

Displays	Mail car, coach, sleeper
Dates open	Late June through August, daily, 9 a.m.-8 p.m.
Admission	Free
Memberships	Write for information.
Nearby attractions	Signal Hill National Historic Park
Address	Government of Newfoundland and Labrador, Department of Development and Tourism, St. John's, NF A1C 5T7
Phone	(800) 563-6353 (Department of Development and Tourism)

NEWFOUNDLAND AND LABRADOR MUSEUM OF TRANSPORTATION

The Newfoundland Transportation Society has begun development of a museum on a 4½-acre site in Pippy Park in St. John's. The collection now includes a mail car, a coach, and a sleeping car from Canadian National Railway's 3'6" gauge Newfoundland lines. The park is on Mount Scio Road in St. John's. There is a restaurant in Pippy Park; food and lodging can be found in the city of St. John's.

Displays	Caboose, baggage car, several passenger cars	**Nearby attractions**	Breton Fisheries and Marine Exhibition Fortress of Louisbourg National Historic Park
Dates open	June-September, daily 9 a.m.-8 p.m.	**Address**	P. O. Box 225, Louisbourg, NS B0A 1M0
Admission	Free		
Memberships	Write for information.	**Phone**	(902) 733-2720
Special events	Annual Reunion (second Sunday of September), "Ceilidh" during the Cape		

SYDNEY & LOUISBURG RAILWAY MUSEUM

The Sydney & Louisburg Railway Historical Society operates a museum in the former S&L station in Louisbourg, Nova Scotia. The station was built in 1895, and several pieces of rolling stock are on display there. Louisbourg is about 22 miles from Sydney, near the eastern tip of Cape Breton Island. Food and lodging are available in Louisbourg.

Displays	School car
Dates open	May 24 through end of September, daily
Admission	Free
Memberships	Write for information.
Nearby attractions	Town Hall, Piano Factory, Benmiller Inn, Blyth Festival
Address	Box 400, Clinton, ON N0M 1L0
Phone	(519) 482-3997

P ♿ ⛩

SCHOOL ON WHEELS 15089

In 1926 the province of Ontario put into service a school car — a coach rebuilt to contain a classroom and living quarters for a teacher. It was an experiment in educating children in remote areas. It was a success, and soon seven such cars were traveling through northern Ontario. In 1982 one of the cars, No. 15089 was discovered in derelict condition. The town of Clinton, home of Fred Sloman, who had taught on that car for 38 years, recognized the value of the car, purchased it, and placed it in the Sloman Memorial Park in Clinton. The car is being restored by a group of volunteers. The park is on Victoria Terrace, off Victoria Street (Route 4) two blocks south of the Canadian National crossing in Clinton. Clinton is 33 miles northwest of Stratford; food and lodging are available in Clinton.

Displays	Steam locomotive, passenger cars, caboose
Dates open	Mid-June through first week of September, daily 9 a.m.-9 p.m.
Admission	Families $2, students (under 19) $1, age 55 and over 65 cents
Nearby attractions	Polar Bear Express, Drury Park
Address	P. O. Box 490, Cochrane, ON P0L 1C0
Phone	(705) 272-4361

P

COCHRANE RAILWAY AND PIONEER MUSEUM

Cochrane, Ontario, was incorporated in 1910 at the junction of two railways, the Temiskaming & Northern Ontario (now Ontario Northland) and the National Transcontinental (now a secondary line of the Canadian National). When a museum of Cochrane's pioneer days was established in 1970 it was appropriate that the railroads be included. Among the museum's display are T&NO 2-8-0 No. 137, a CN caboose, a CN baggage car housing displays of pioneer life, and a CN coach that contains a model railroad and numerous railroad artifacts. The museum is at the Ontario Northland-VIA station at Railway Street and Seventh Avenue in Cochrane. Food and lodging are available nearby.

Displays	2 stations, 2 steam locomotives, caboose, artifacts
Dates open	May 24-June, weekends; July-Labor Day, daily; Labor Day-Thanksgiving (October 12), weekends, noon-5 p.m.
Admission	Adults $2; children under 13, 50 cents. Checks accepted. Group discounts available.
Memberships	Write for information.
Nearby attractions	Niagara Falls, Willowby Museum, Battlefield Museum
Address	P. O. Box 355, Fort Erie, ON L2A 5M1
Phone	(416) 871-1412, 871-3047 for recorded information

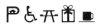

FORT ERIE RAILROAD MUSEUM

The Fort Erie Railroad Museum has two station buildings originally belonging to the Grand Trunk Railway: One is GT's first station in Fort Erie, built in 1873; the other (built in 1891) is from Ridgeway, Ontario, 8 miles away. On display at the museum are Canadian National 4-8-4 6218, a CN caboose, a Porter fireless locomotive, and numerous artifacts. The museum is in Oakes Park at Central Avenue a short distance northwest of the west end of the Peace Bridge, which connects Fort Erie, Ont., with Buffalo, New York. Food and lodging are available nearby.

Displays	Steam locomotive, 2 coaches, caboose, HO gauge model railroad
Dates open	Mid- to late June, Monday-Saturday 1-5 p.m.; July 1-Labor Day, daily noon-5
Admission	Free; donations welcome
Memberships	Write for information.
Nearby attractions	Heritage Boat Tour, hunting, fishing
Address	88 Riverside Drive, Kapuskasing, ON P5N 1B3
Phone	(705) 335-5443; 335-2341 for recorded information

RON MOREL MEMORIAL MUSEUM

The Ron Morel Memorial Museum has displays of pioneer and railroad memorabilia, fur trading exhibits, and an HO gauge model railroad housed in two Canadian National coaches and a caboose. A Canadian National 4-6-2 is also on display. The museum is located at the Canadian National station on Route 11 in Kapuskasing. Food and lodging are available in Kapuskasing.

Displays	7 steam locomotives
Dates open	May 1-Labor Day, daily 10 a.m.-8 p.m.; remainder of the year open 9-5, closed Mondays, but open on Mondays that are holidays
Admission	Free
Nearby attractions	Parliament buildings, Bytown Museum
Address	1867 St. Laurent Boulevard, Ottawa, ON K1A 0M8
Phone	(613) 998-4566

NATIONAL MUSEUM OF SCIENCE AND TECHNOLOGY

Among the displays in Ottawa's National Museum of Science and Technology are seven steam locomotives: Hudsons and Northerns from both Canadian National and Canadian Pacific plus a CP 4-6-0, a CN 4-4-0, and a CN 0-6-0T. Also on display are several passenger cars.

The museum is southeast of downtown Ottawa on St. Laurent Boulevard south of Queensway East (Route 417). City buses can take you there from downtown or the VIA station — the museum is about 2 miles from the VIA station. The museum has a cafeteria, and there are several fast-food restaurants within walking distance. Lodging is available in Ottawa.

In recent years the museum has operated excursion trains to the town of Wakefield, Quebec, about 18 miles away, using Canadian Pacific 4-6-2 No. 1201. At press time information on whether such trains would run in 1987 was unavailable.

Locomotives	2 diesel
Cars	2 open cars, 1 caboose
Displays	Business car, cabooses, Burro crane, work equipment
Schedule	May, September, and October, weekends and holidays hourly from 1 to 4 p.m.; June, weekends 1-5; July and August, Saturdays 1-5, Sundays 12-5, Wednesday-Friday 1 and 3; November and December until Christmas, Sundays at 1 and 3. Charter trips available.
Fares	Adults $4, children under 13 $2. Checks and credit cards accepted. Group discounts available.
Memberships	Write for information.
Special events	Santa Claus trains
Nearby attractions	Pinafore Park Railroad, Village of Sparta, monument to Jumbo the elephant
Address	Box 549, Port Stanley, ON N0L 2A0
Phone	(519) 782-9993

PORT STANLEY TERMINAL RAIL

The London & Port Stanley, an electric railway connecting London, Ontario, with Lake Erie at Port Stanley, became part of Canadian National in 1966. The portion of the line between St. Thomas and Port Stanley was abandoned, but in 1983 a 3-mile segment from Port Stanley to Union was returned to excursion service as Port Stanley Terminal Rail. Trains run from a station next to Kettle Creek and make a 45-minute round trip. Food and lodging are available in Port Stanley, about 9 miles south of St. Thomas on Route 4.

Cars	Streetcars and interurbans
Displays	Cars under restoration
Dates open	Mid-May to mid-October, weekends and holidays 11 a.m.-5 p.m.; July and August, daily 11-5. Charters available.
Admission	Adults $3, children 3-12 $1.50, age 65 and over $1.50. Higher for special events; lower when cars are not operating. Admission includes unlimited rides. Credit cards accepted. Group discounts available.
Memberships	Write for information.
Special events	Extravaganzas (Sundays in late June and late September), Christmas Fiesta (early December)
Nearby attractions	Ontario Agriculture Museum, Rockwood Conservation Area
Address	Box 121, Station A, Scarboro, ON M1K 5B9
Phone	(519) 856-9802

Brian C. Nickle

HALTON COUNTY RADIAL RAILWAY MUSEUM

The Halton County Radial Railway Museum (in Ontario interurbans were called "radial railways") was begun in 1953 when several enthusiasts saved a historic Toronto streetcar from being scrapped. The group acquired a section of the roadbed of a defunct Toronto-Guelph interurban line, and track construction began in 1961, about the time the group organized as the Ontario Electric Railway Historical Association. The track is the same gauge as the Toronto streetcar system, 4'10⅞" — just about 1.5 meters. The collection includes more than a dozen operating streetcars and interurbans and numerous pieces of freight and work equipment. The museum offers a 20-minute round trip ride over 1¼ miles of track; admission to the museum includes unlimited rides. To reach the museum from Toronto and Hamilton, take Queen Elizabeth Way to the Guelph Line exit in Burlington, then follow Guelph Line northwest 22 miles to the museum. From London, take Exit 312 (Guelph Line) from Highway 401, then go 9 miles northwest to the museum. Food can be found in Rockwood; lodging in Guelph.

Locomotives	1 diesel
Cars	1 coach converted from an open streetcar
Dates open	May 15-October 15, weekends 1 p.m.to sunset. Charter trips available.
Fares	Adults $1; children 2-11, 50 cents. Checks accepted. Group discounts available.
Nearby attractions	Storybook Gardens, Port Stanley Terminal Rail, monument to Jumbo the elephant
Address	477 Charlotte Street, London, ON N5W 4A5
Phone	(519) 455-2852

PINAFORE PARK RAILROAD

Pinafore Park is a 90-acre attraction in St. Thomas, Ontario, which includes picnic tables, gardens, woods, tame deer — and a 1-mile loop of narrow gauge track, the Pinafore Park Railroad. The train consists of a 25-ton 4-wheel diesel that originally worked in Newfoundland and an excursion coach that was rebuilt from an open streetcar. The ride takes about 10 minutes. Pinafore Park is southeast of the intersection of Highways 3 and 4, near the crossing of the CSX (ex-Chesapeake & Ohio) and Canadian National's ex-London & Port Stanley line. Food and lodging are available in St. Thomas.

Locomotives	Diesels
Cars	Air conditioned coaches, dining car. Private cars available for charter.
Schedule	Agawa Canyon: early June-Columbus Day (Thanksgiving in Canada), daily leave Sault Ste. Marie 8 a.m., at Agawa Canyon 11:30-1:30, arrive Sault Ste. Marie 5 p.m. Hearst: late May-Columbus Day, leave Sault Ste. Marie 9:30 a.m. daily except Monday, arrive Hearst 7:15 p.m., leave Hearst 8:15 a.m. daily except Tuesday, arrive Sault Ste. Marie 6:10 p.m.; remainder of the year, leave Sault Ste. Marie 8:30 a.m. Friday, Saturday, and Sunday, arrive Hearst 5:50 p.m., leave Hearst 7:15 a.m. Saturday, Sunday, and Monday, arrive Sault Ste. Marie 4:30 p.m.
Fares	Round trip to Agawa Canyon: adults $29, children 5 through high school $14.50 (under 5 free), age 60 and over during June $20. Group discounts available. Round trip to Hearst: adults $72, children under 12 $36.
Nearby attractions	Soo Locks tours
Address	129 Bay Street, Sault Ste. Marie, ON P6A 1W7
Phone	(705) 254-4331

MODEL RAILROADER: Jim Hediger

ALGOMA CENTRAL RAILWAY

The Algoma Central Railway is a common carrier extending 297 miles north from Sault Ste. Marie, Ontario, to Hearst. Its principal business is carrying iron ore and forest products, but it operates excursion trains over its entire main line. The most popular trip is a one-day ride from Sault Ste. Marie 114 miles north through forests and along lakes and rivers to spectacular Agawa Canyon and return. A tour of the entire line requires two days and an overnight stay in Hearst.

The Agawa Canyon train carries a dining car offering hot meals, sandwiches, snacks, and box lunches. During summer the Hearst train offers take-out food service except Monday and Tuesday between Sault Ste. Marie and Eton, 120 miles. During the remainder of the year the Hearst train carries a dining car Saturdays and Sundays between Sault Ste. Marie and Eton.

Advance reservations are not accepted, but tickets may be purchased between 7 a.m. and 7 p.m. the day before departure at the station in Sault Ste. Marie. The remaining tickets are sold the next morning from 7 to 8. Advance purchase is advised during the fall foliage season. Handicapped persons can be accommodated with advance notice. Food and lodging are available within walking distance of the stations at Sault Ste. Marie and Hearst.

Displays	Diesel switcher, freight cars, artifacts
Dates open	May-August, daily 9 a.m.-5 p.m.; September, weekends 10-4; October, Sundays 10-4
Admission	Free, donations welcome
Memberships	$5 per year
Nearby attractions	Rideau Canal, Hershey Chocolate plant
Address	P. O. Box 962, Smiths Falls, ON K7A 5A5
Phone	(613) 283-1334, 283-5964

P &

SMITHS FALLS RAILWAY MUSEUM

The Rideau Valley Division of the Canadian Railroad Historical Association maintains a museum in the former Canadian National (earlier, Canadian Northern) station at Smiths Falls, Ontario. The building was constructed in 1914; it was designated a National Historic Site in 1985. On display are several freight cars and ex-Canadian Pacific diesel switcher No. 6591, an S3 built by Montreal Locomotive Works. Inside the station are artifacts and memorabilia. The museum is at William and Church Streets on the west side of Smiths Falls, about six blocks from the Canadian Pacific station used by VIA's Ottawa-Toronto trains. There are restaurants within a few blocks of the museum, and lodging is available in Smiths Falls. Smiths Falls is about 40 miles south of Ottawa and 30 miles northwest of Brockville.

Displays	Station, photos, artifacts
Dates open	Mid-June to Labor Day, daily 10 a.m.-6 p.m.
Admission	Individuals free, donations welcome; $1 per person for bus tours
Memberships	Write for information.
Nearby attractions	East Point Lighthouse, Basin Head Fisheries Museum, beaches, deep-sea fishing
Address	Elmira, PE C0A 1K0
Phone	(902) 357-2481

P & 🎁

ELMIRA RAILWAY MUSEUM

The Prince Edward Island Railway was built in the early 1870s with a track gauge of 42 inches. It was taken over by the Canadian government soon after Prince Edward Island became part of Canada in 1873 and eventually became part of Canadian National Railways. It was standard-gauged in the 1920s and given a mainland connection by means of ferries between Borden and Cape Tormentine, New Brunswick. Passenger service was discontinued about 1970, but freight service continues today. The station at Elmira, easternmost point of the railroad, has become a museum illustrating the development and operation of railroads on Prince Edward Island. Elmira is on Route 16A at the eastern tip of Prince Edward Island. The nearest restaurant is about 5 miles away; the nearest motel, 10 miles away.

Locomotives	3 diesel, 1 steam, 1 RDC
Cars	Steel combination car
Displays	More than 80 locomotives, cars, and streetcars
Dates open	May 2-October 25, 1987, daily 9 a.m.-5 p.m.
Admission	Adults $3.25, children 4-12 $1.75 (children under 6 must be accompanied by adults), age 60 and over $2. Discounts available to groups of 10 or more with reservations.
Memberships	Write for information.
Special events	Members Day (June 21, 1987), Canada Day (July 1), Railway Days (July 19), Model Railway Competition (September 6)
Nearby attractions	Montreal, St. Lawrence Seaway Locks
Address	P. O. Box 148, St. Constant, PQ J0L 1X0
Phone	(514) 638-1522; 632-2410 for recorded information

Sandy Worthen

CANADIAN RAILWAY MUSEUM

The Canadian Railway Museum, operated by the Canadian Railroad Historical Association, is the largest collection of railroad and street railway equipment in Canada. Included are 4-6-4s from Canadian National and Canadian Pacific, a CN 2-10-2 and a CP 2-10-4, several historic diesels, CP 4-4-0 No. 144, the oldest Canadian-built locomotive in existence (built in 1886 by the CP), and an operating replica of the *John Molson*, a locomotive built in 1849 for the Champlain & St. Lawrence Rail Road. The museum offers streetcar rides on a 1-mile loop of track around the property and train rides over a ¾-mile stretch of track. Other museum activities include a series of art exhibitions and a puppet theater.

The museum is about 30 minutes from downtown Montreal. To reach the museum, follow Route 132 (Boulevard Taschereau) along the south shore of the St. Lawrence River between Route 15 and the Mercier Bridge to Route 209, then follow 209 a mile south. Restaurants and lodging can be found nearby.

St. Constant

Displays	Caboose, motor car, station	**Memberships**	Write for information.
Dates open	Late May to Labor Day weekend, Saturdays to mid-June, then daily 10 a.m.-6 p.m.	**Nearby attractions**	Moose Mountain Provincial Park, Cannington Manor Historic Park
		Address	Box 840, Carlyle, SK S0C 0R0
Admission	Adults 50 cents; families $2. Checks accepted.	**Phone**	(306) 453-2266

⚐ ♿ ⊼ 🎁

RUSTY RELIC MUSEUM

The Rusty Relic Museum is primarily a museum of pioneer days in Saskatchewan, but it is housed in a former Canadian National station and a Canadian Pacific caboose and a CN motor car are on display outside. The museum is near the Canadian Pacific tracks at Third Street West and Railway Avenue in Carlyle. Food and lodging are available in Carlyle, which is in southeast Saskatchewan about 60 miles north of the U. S. border and 40 miles west of the Manitoba border.

Dates open	June-August, daily 8 a.m.-8 p.m.; rest of the year Tuesday-Sunday 9-5
Schedule	Steam locomotive operates Sundays and holiday Mondays in summer.
Admission	Adults $2.50; children under 16, 75 cents (preschool free); age 65 and over $1.50. Checks accepted. Discount available for groups of 10 adults or more.
Memberships	Write for information.
Nearby attractions	Wild Animal Park, Pioneer Village Museum
Address	Box 185, Moose Jaw, SK S6H 4N8
Phone	(306) 693-6556

⚐ ♿ ⊼ 🎁

SASKATCHEWAN WESTERN DEVELOPMENT MUSEUM

The Moose Jaw branch of the Saskatchewan Western Development Museums specializes in transportation of all types, from birchbark canoes to airplanes, with some emphasis on the role of the railroad in opening western Canada. On the museum grounds is a short railroad with a steam locomotive that operates on summer Sundays. The museum is at 50 Diefenbaker Drive in Moose Jaw, southeast of the intersection of the Trans Canada Highway Bypass and Main Street (Route 2). Food and lodging are available nearby.

Locomotives	Diesels: GP28s, GP38-2s, GP40s, GP40-2s
Cars	Conventional streamlined cars: coaches, dome coaches, lounge, dining car
Schedule	The *Vista Train* leaves Chihuahua daily at 7 a.m. and Los Mochis daily at 6 a.m. The 405-mile trip takes almost 14 hours. The trains meet at Divisadero Barrancas, the station at the rim of Copper Canyon. Additional

local services are offered.

Fares	Because of the fluctuation of the Mexican peso it is impossible to state the fare precisely; at press time round trip on the Vista Train cost approximately $50.
Address	Ferrocarril de Chihuahua al Pacifico, P. O. Box 46, Chihuahua, Chih., Mexico
Phone	2-22-84

CHIHUAHUA PACIFIC RAILWAY (Ferrocarril de Chihuahua al Pacifico)

Like the Alaska Railroad in the United States, the Chihuahua Pacific is a common-carrier freight and passenger railroad. It is best known for the *Copper Canyon Express*, which runs between the city of Chihuahua, south of El Paso, Texas, and Los Mochis, on the shore of the Gulf of California. West of Chihuahua the line traverses high plains and then forested country before reaching the Continental Divide. Trains pause for sightseeing at the rim of Copper Canyon. The western slope of the Sierra Madre is some of the wildest topography in North America, and the scenery is worth riding through twice.

It's easiest to ride the line as a round trip from Chihuahua. The trip takes most of a week: a day from the border at El Paso or Presido, Tex., to Chihuahua; an entire day to Los Mochis; a day there out of deference to the late-evening arrival and the early-morning departure; a day back to Chihuahua; and a day from there to the border. You might want to plan a 24-hour stopover at one of the lodges or hotels the railroad operates near Copper Canyon. Chihuahua has air service from Ciudad Juarez, Tijuana, and San Antonio. National Railways of Mexico operates three trains a day between Ciudad Juarez and Chihuahua — 221 miles, 4 hours. The two railroads use different stations in Chihuahua. Starting and ending your trip at Los Mochis is preferable only if you are already on the west coast of Mexico. Highway mileages from Tucson, Arizona, to Los Mochis and Chihuahua are virtually the same.

Reservations are required. Write to the Chihuahua Pacific office in Chihuahua at least a month in advance of your trip.

Locomotives	1 steam
Cars	2 wooden coaches
Address	Club Amigos del Ferrocarril, A. C., Apdo. Postal 7-1372, Mexico 7, D. F., Mexico
Phone	379-17-62

CLUB AMIGOS DEL FERROCARRIL

The Club Amigos del Ferrocarril (Friends of the Railroad) and the state of Morelos jointly operate a stretch of 3-foot-gauge track at Cuautla, about 50 miles south of Mexico City. The club owns 75 kilometers (about 45 miles) of the track from Cuautla to Amecameca at the base of Mount Popocateptl. The line was once part of the Interoceanic Railway route from Mexico City to Puebla. The locomotive is 2-8-0 No. 279, built in 1921 by Baldwin Locomotive Works; passengers ride in a pair of wooden coaches.

VISITING A TOURIST RAILROAD OR MUSEUM

Visiting a railroad museum or a tourist line is an enjoyable way to spend an afternoon — and you'll have a better time if you are prepared for the conditions you will encounter. Most museums are out in the open. Visitors (and the exhibits) have little protection from the weather. Further, summer is the prime season for most railroad museums. It will be hot and sunny. Riding a train in the mountains, though, you'll want to be ready for cool weather and maybe rain.

Walking surfaces at the museums are more often dirt roads and paths and gravel track areas than they are pavement. Choose your footwear with that in mind. Conditions are usually less than ideal for wheelchairs and strollers and for those who have difficulty walking. Safety rule: Always step over the rails, not on them.

A visit to a railroad museum is a good family activity. Remember that operating museums are working railroads, which means "Any time is train time." Keep an eye on your children, and consider the attention spans of your children and of adults who may not share your depth of enthusiasm. Rather than start by riding the train or streetcar and then browse through the exhibits until everyone is tired, plan to look at some exhibits, take the ride (you'll welcome the chance to sit down, particularly if you've had to carry or lift small kids), then look at more exhibits.

A break for refreshments is another good way to perk up sagging youngsters and ward off your own "museum feet." Many of the museums offer refreshment facilities, which can range from a soft drink machine to a small restaurant. Some have picnic areas, too — but if you plan a cookout, ask in advance. Since much historic railroad rolling stock is wood, museums may be reluctant to allow fires nearby.

Riding a train is another good family experience, and another place to make sure children aren't hanging out the windows or jumping from car to car (the same goes for adults). Children who have known only the automobile may be amazed that something the size of a train can move and that there can be room to move around, get a drink of water, or even go to the bathroom. (It's at the end of the car, and it's a good idea to ask if it's usable — some tourist railroads consider toilet facilities unnecessary for a 30-minute ride.)

Ironically most railroad museums are accessible only by car. Few railroad museums and tourist railroads are fortunate enough to have Amtrak or even a city bus stop at their door. The few exceptions are noted in the body of the book, such as the California State Railroad Museum at Sacramento and the Baltimore Streetcar Museum, which are within easy walking distance of Amtrak stations. Most museums and tourist railroads offer free parking.

Most museums welcome groups and offer guided tours. Some can even accommodate midweek visits by groups of students or retired persons. Advance notice is necessary for groups. If you have to make a long trip to a museum, call or write to confirm schedules — in the latter case as a courtesy enclose a stamped, self-addressed envelope.

Most of the railroad museums in this book are nonprofit organizations staffed by volunteers who give time to the museum, and they are financed through admission charges, fares, profits from refreshment and souvenir sales, and donations from visitors and from those same volunteers who keep the museum running.

Most museums make a point of being open on holidays; for others it's just the opposite. Here are the 1987 and 1988 dates of the holidays mentioned in the schedules throughout the book.

	1987	1988
New Year's Day	January 1	January 1
Easter	April 19	April 3
Memorial Day	May 25	May 30
Independence Day	July 4	July 4
Labor Day	September 7	September 5
Columbus Day	October 12	October 10
Thanksgiving (Canada)	October 12	October 10
Thanksgiving (U. S.)	November 26	November 24
Christmas Eve	December 24	December 24
Christmas	December 25	December 25

INDEX

SAVINGS COUPON

Adults: $1.00 off fare
Children: 50¢ off fare
Valid during 1987

PACIFIC SOUTHWEST RWY MUSEUM
Campo, California

SAVINGS COUPON

Adults: 60¢ off admission
Age 65 and over: 60¢ off admission
Age 5-11: 10¢ off admission
Age 12-18: 30¢ off admission
Valid during 1987

FORNEY TRANSPORTATION MUSEUM
Denver, Colorado

SAVINGS COUPON

50¢ off fare
Valid during 1987

WILMINGTON & WESTERN RR
Wilmington, Delaware

SAVINGS COUPON

Adults: $1.00 off fare
Children: 50¢ off fare
Valid during 1987

ROARING CAMP & BIG TREES RR
Felton, California

SAVINGS COUPON

50¢ off fare
Charters: 10% off
Valid during 1987

HOUSATONIC RAIL ROAD
Canaan, Connecticut

SAVINGS COUPON

Adults: $1.00 off fare
Age 60 and over: $1.00 off fare
Children: 50¢ off fare
Valid during 1987

GOLD COAST RR MUSEUM
Miami, Florida

SAVINGS COUPON

25¢ off admission
Valid during 1987

LOMITA RAILROAD MUSEUM
Lomita, California

SAVINGS COUPON

Adults: 50¢ off fare
Age 62 and over: $1.00 off fare
Children: 50¢ off fare
Valid during 1987

CONNECTICUT TROLLEY MUSEUM
East Windsor, Connecticut

SAVINGS COUPON

Adults: $1.00 off admission
Age 65 and over: $1.00 off admission
Valid during 1987

BIG SHANTY MUSEUM
Kennesaw, Georgia

SAVINGS COUPON

Adults: 50¢ off fare
Children: 25¢ off fare
Valid during 1987

ROYAL GORGE SCENIC RWY
Canon City, Colorado

SAVINGS COUPON

10% off admission
Valid during 1987

VALLEY RAILROAD
Essex, Connecticut

SAVINGS COUPON

Adults: 50¢ off admission
Children: 25¢ off admission
Valid during 1987

OKEFENOKEE HERITAGE CENTER
Waycross, Georgia

GUIDE TO TOURIST RAILROADS

KALMBACH **K** BOOKS

GUIDE TO TOURIST RAILROADS

KALMBACH **K** BOOKS

GUIDE TO TOURIST RAILROADS

KALMBACH **K** BOOKS

GUIDE TO TOURIST RAILROADS

KALMBACH **K** BOOKS

GUIDE TO TOURIST RAILROADS

KALMBACH **K** BOOKS

GUIDE TO TOURIST RAILROADS

KALMBACH **K** BOOKS

GUIDE TO TOURIST RAILROADS

KALMBACH **K** BOOKS

GUIDE TO TOURIST RAILROADS

KALMBACH **K** BOOKS

GUIDE TO TOURIST RAILROADS

KALMBACH **K** BOOKS

GUIDE TO TOURIST RAILROADS

KALMBACH **K** BOOKS

GUIDE TO TOURIST RAILROADS

KALMBACH **K** BOOKS

GUIDE TO TOURIST RAILROADS

KALMBACH **K** BOOKS

SAVINGS COUPON

Adults: 50¢ off admission
Children: 50¢ off admission
Valid during 1987

MONTICELLO RWY MUSEUM
Monticello, Illinois

SAVINGS COUPON

Adults: 50¢ off fare
Children: 25¢ off fare
Valid during 1987

INDIANA TRANSPORTATION MUSEUM
Noblesville, Indiana

SAVINGS COUPON

Adults: $1.00 off fare
Age 60 and over: $1.00 off fare
Children: 50¢ off fare
Valid during 1987

MARYLAND MIDLAND RWY
Union Bridge, Maryland

SAVINGS COUPON

50¢ off admission
Valid during 1987

ILLINOIS RWY MUSEUM
Union, Illinois

SAVINGS COUPON

Adults: $1.00 off admission
Age 65 and over: 50¢ off admission
Children: 50¢ off admission
Valid during 1987

KENTUCKY RWY MUSEUM
Louisville, Kentucky

SAVINGS COUPON

Adults: $1.00 off fare
Age 62 and over: $1.00 off fare
Valid during 1987

CAPE COD & HYANNIS RR
Hyannis, Massachusetts

SAVINGS COUPON

Adults: $1.00 off fare
Valid during 1987

WHITEWATER VALLEY RR
Connersville, Indiana

SAVINGS COUPON

Adults: 50¢ off admission
Children: 25¢ off admission
Valid during 1987

LOUISIANA STATE RR MUSEUM
Kenner, Louisiana

SAVINGS COUPON

50¢ off fare
Valid during 1987

BERKSHIRE SCENIC RWY MUSEUM
Lee, Massachusetts

SAVINGS COUPON

$1.00 off fare
Valid during 1987

INDIANA RWY MUSEUM
French Lick, Indiana

SAVINGS COUPON

One free ride with paid fare
of equal or greater value
Valid during 1987

BALTIMORE STREETCAR MUSEUM
Baltimore, Maryland

SAVINGS COUPON

Adults: 50¢ off admission
Age 65 and over: 50¢ off admission
Children: 25¢ off admission
Valid during 1987

A&D TOY-TRAIN VILLAGE
& RR MUSEUM
Middleboro, Massachusetts

GUIDE TO TOURIST RAILROADS

KALMBACH BOOKS

GUIDE TO TOURIST RAILROADS

KALMBACH BOOKS

GUIDE TO TOURIST RAILROADS

KALMBACH BOOKS

GUIDE TO TOURIST RAILROADS

KALMBACH BOOKS

GUIDE TO TOURIST RAILROADS

KALMBACH BOOKS

GUIDE TO TOURIST RAILROADS

KALMBACH BOOKS

GUIDE TO TOURIST RAILROADS

KALMBACH BOOKS

GUIDE TO TOURIST RAILROADS

KALMBACH BOOKS

GUIDE TO TOURIST RAILROADS

KALMBACH BOOKS

GUIDE TO TOURIST RAILROADS

KALMBACH BOOKS

GUIDE TO TOURIST RAILROADS

KALMBACH BOOKS

GUIDE TO TOURIST RAILROADS

KALMBACH BOOKS

SAVINGS COUPON

$1.00 off admission
Valid during 1987

EDAVILLE RR
South Carver, Massachusetts

SAVINGS COUPON

Adults: $1.00 off fare
Age 65 and over: $1.00 off fare
Children: 50¢ off fare
Valid during 1987

LEELANAU SCENIC RR
Traverse City, Michigan

SAVINGS COUPON

$1.00 discount on books purchased
from museum gift shop
Valid during 1987

WHIPPANY RWY MUSEUM
Whippany, New Jersey

SAVINGS COUPON

Adults: $1.20 off admission
Age 60 and over: $1.00 off admission
Children: 80¢ off admission
Valid during 1987

HUCKLEBERRY RR
Flint, Michigan

SAVINGS COUPON

$1.00 off fare
Valid during 1987

MAGNOLIA STATE RWY
Amory, Mississippi

SAVINGS COUPON

Adults: 50¢ off fare
Senior citizens: 50¢ off fare
Children: 25¢ off fare
Valid during 1987

DELAWARE & ULSTER RAIL RIDE
Arkville, New York

SAVINGS COUPON

Adults: $1.00 off fare
Children: 50¢ off fare
Valid during 1987

MICHIGAN TRANSIT MUSEUM
Mt. Clemens, Michigan

SAVINGS COUPON

50¢ off fare
Valid through June 26, 1988

WABASH, FRISCO & PACIFIC
Glencoe, Missouri

SAVINGS COUPON

$1.00 off fare
Valid during 1987

TIOGA CENTRAL RAIL EXCURSIONS
Owego, New York

SAVINGS COUPON

Adults: 50¢ off fare
Children: 50¢ off fare
Valid during 1987

TOONERVILLE TROLLEY
Soo Junction, Michigan

SAVINGS COUPON

$1.00 off fare
Valid during 1987

ST. LOUIS, IRON MOUNTAIN
& SOUTHERN RAILWAY
Jackson, Missouri

SAVINGS COUPON

Adults: 50¢ off admission
Children: 25¢ off admission
Valid during 1987

NEW YORK MUSEUM
OF TRANSPORTATION
West Henrietta, New York

GUIDE TO TOURIST RAILROADS

KALMBACH **K** BOOKS.

GUIDE TO TOURIST RAILROADS

KALMBACH **K** BOOKS.

GUIDE TO TOURIST RAILROADS

KALMBACH **K** BOOKS.

GUIDE TO TOURIST RAILROADS

KALMBACH **K** BOOKS.

GUIDE TO TOURIST RAILROADS

KALMBACH **K** BOOKS.

GUIDE TO TOURIST RAILROADS

KALMBACH **K** BOOKS.

GUIDE TO TOURIST RAILROADS

KALMBACH **K** BOOKS.

GUIDE TO TOURIST RAILROADS

KALMBACH **K** BOOKS.

GUIDE TO TOURIST RAILROADS

KALMBACH **K** BOOKS.

GUIDE TO TOURIST RAILROADS

KALMBACH **K** BOOKS.

GUIDE TO TOURIST RAILROADS

KALMBACH **K** BOOKS.

SAVINGS COUPON

$1.00 off admission
Valid during 1987

TWEETSIE RR
Blowing Rock, North Carolina

SAVINGS COUPON

Adults: 50¢ off admission
Age 60 and over: 50¢ off admission
Children: 25¢ off admission
Families: $1.00 off admission

Valid during 1987

RAILROADER'S MEMORIAL MUSEUM
Altoona, Pennsylvania

SAVINGS COUPON

Adults: 50¢ off fare
Age 60 and over: 50¢ off fare
Children: 25¢ off fare

Valid during 1987

OIL CREEK & TITUSVILLE RR
Oil City, Pennsylvania

SAVINGS COUPON

Adults: $1.00 off fare
Children: 50¢ off fare

Valid during 1987

INDIANA & OHIO RR
Mason, Ohio

SAVINGS COUPON

50¢ off fare
Valid during 1987

GETTYSBURG RR
Gettysburg, Pennsylvania

SAVINGS COUPON

Two tickets for the price of one
Valid during 1987

SHADE GAP ELECTRIC RWY
Orbisonia, Pennsylvania

SAVINGS COUPON

50¢ off fare
Valid during 1987

BUCKEYE CENTRAL SCENIC RR
Newark, Ohio

SAVINGS COUPON

Adults: 50¢ off fare
Children: 25¢ off fare

Valid during 1987

WANAMAKER, KEMPTON & SOUTHERN
Kempton, Pennsylvania

SAVINGS COUPON

50¢ off admission
Valid during 1987

FRANKLIN INSTITUTE
SCIENCE MUSEUM
Philadelphia, Pennsylvania

SAVINGS COUPON

$1.00 off admission
$2.50 off family rate
Valid during 1987

TROLLEY PARK
Glenwood, Oregon

SAVINGS COUPON

Adults: 50¢ off fare
Age 65 and over: $1.00 off fare
Children: 50¢ off fare

Valid during 1987

NEW HOPE STEAM RWY
New Hope, Pennsylvania

SAVINGS COUPON

Adults: 25¢ off fare
Children: 15¢ off fare

Valid during 1987

PENNS LANDING TROLLEY
Philadelphia, Pennsylvania

GUIDE TO TOURIST RAILROADS

KALMBACH **K** BOOKS

GUIDE TO TOURIST RAILROADS

KALMBACH **K** BOOKS

GUIDE TO TOURIST RAILROADS

KALMBACH **K** BOOKS

GUIDE TO TOURIST RAILROADS

KALMBACH **K** BOOKS

GUIDE TO TOURIST RAILROADS

KALMBACH **K** BOOKS

GUIDE TO TOURIST RAILROADS

KALMBACH **K** BOOKS

GUIDE TO TOURIST RAILROADS

KALMBACH **K** BOOKS

GUIDE TO TOURIST RAILROADS

KALMBACH **K** BOOKS

GUIDE TO TOURIST RAILROADS

KALMBACH **K** BOOKS

GUIDE TO TOURIST RAILROADS

KALMBACH **K** BOOKS

GUIDE TO TOURIST RAILROADS

KALMBACH **K** BOOKS

GUIDE TO TOURIST RAILROADS

KALMBACH **K** BOOKS

SAVINGS COUPON

Adults: $1.50 off
Age 65 and over: 50¢ off
Children: 50¢ off
Scranton-Moscow, Pa., fare
Valid during 1987

STEAMTOWN USA
Scranton, Pennsylvania

SAVINGS COUPON

$1.00 off fare
$1.00 off family ticket
Valid during 1987

OLD COLONY & NEWPORT RWY
Newport, Rhode Island

SAVINGS COUPON

Adults: $1.00 off fare
Senior citizens: $2.00 off fare
Children: 50¢ off fare
Valid during 1987

HEBER CREEPER
Heber City, Utah

SAVINGS COUPON

Adults: 25¢ off each admission
(Limit 6 to a party)
Valid during 1987

TOY TRAIN MUSEUM
Strasburg, Pennsylvania

SAVINGS COUPON

Adults: $1.00 off admission
Children: 50¢ off admission
Good for one person only
Valid during 1987

TENNESSEE VALLEY RR MUSEUM
Chattanooga, Tennessee

SAVINGS COUPON

Adults: 45¢ off fare
Valid during 1987

ROCK OF AGES
Barre, Vermont

SAVINGS COUPON

Adults: $1.00 off fare
Children: $1.00 off fare
Not valid for senior citizen fares
Valid during 1987

BLUE MOUNTAIN & READING RR
Temple, Pennsylvania

SAVINGS COUPON

$1.00 off admission
Valid during 1987

THE RAILROAD MUSEUM
Galveston, Texas

SAVINGS COUPON

Adults: 70¢ off fare
Age 55 and over: 70¢ off fare
Children: 50¢ off fare
Valid during 1987

GREEN MOUNTAIN RR
Bellows Falls, Vermont

SAVINGS COUPON

Adults: 50¢ off fare
Children: 25¢ off fare
Valid during 1987

ARDEN TROLLEY MUSEUM
Washington, Pennsylvania

SAVINGS COUPON

50¢ off fare
Valid during 1987

JEFFERSON & CYPRESS BAYOU RR
Jefferson, Texas

SAVINGS COUPON

50¢ off admission
Valid during 1987

SHELBURNE MUSEUM
Shelburne, Vermont

GUIDE TO TOURIST RAILROADS

KALMBACH BOOKS

GUIDE TO TOURIST RAILROADS

KALMBACH BOOKS

GUIDE TO TOURIST RAILROADS

KALMBACH BOOKS

GUIDE TO TOURIST RAILROADS

KALMBACH BOOKS

GUIDE TO TOURIST RAILROADS

KALMBACH BOOKS

GUIDE TO TOURIST RAILROADS

KALMBACH BOOKS

GUIDE TO TOURIST RAILROADS

KALMBACH BOOKS

GUIDE TO TOURIST RAILROADS

KALMBACH BOOKS

GUIDE TO TOURIST RAILROADS

KALMBACH BOOKS

GUIDE TO TOURIST RAILROADS

KALMBACH BOOKS

GUIDE TO TOURIST RAILROADS

KALMBACH BOOKS

GUIDE TO TOURIST RAILROADS

KALMBACH BOOKS

GUIDE TO TOURIST RAILROADS

KALMBACH **K**BOOKS

GUIDE TO TOURIST RAILROADS

KALMBACH **K**BOOKS

GUIDE TO TOURIST RAILROADS

KALMBACH **K**BOOKS

GUIDE TO TOURIST RAILROADS

KALMBACH **K**BOOKS

GUIDE TO TOURIST RAILROADS

KALMBACH **K**BOOKS

GUIDE TO TOURIST RAILROADS

KALMBACH **K**BOOKS

GUIDE TO TOURIST RAILROADS

KALMBACH **K**BOOKS

GUIDE TO TOURIST RAILROADS

KALMBACH **K**BOOKS

GUIDE TO TOURIST RAILROADS

KALMBACH **K**BOOKS

GUIDE TO TOURIST RAILROADS

KALMBACH **K**BOOKS

GUIDE TO TOURIST RAILROADS

KALMBACH **K**BOOKS

GUIDE TO TOURIST RAILROADS

KALMBACH **K**BOOKS